Tragedy in Small Town Tennessee,

The Maury County Jail Fire

By the same author

Loving Your Job as a Debt Collector

The "Perfect" Female;
A Guide Toward Truth, Weight Loss, and Physical Health

The "Perfect" Female
Ladies Bible-Class Workbook

My Story of Trauma and PTSD

The Columbia Breakfast Rotary Club,
Service Above Self

ISBN: 9781982958060

Dedicated to the memory of forty-two precious souls who lost their lives in the Maury County Jail Fire on June 26, 1977, and to the numerous family members who were left behind.

Tragedy in Small Town Tennessee,

The Maury County Jail Fire

Acknowledgements: I offer my most sincere thanks to each person listed below who shared their memories. The titles shown reflect the June, 1977 time-period.

- Jerry Wayne Dickey, Criminal Investigator

- William Duke, Deputy

- Bob Farmer, Chief Deputy

- Harvey Fischer, Police Officer

- James George Hanvy, Off-Duty Field Deputy

- Don Martin, Firefighter

- Janet Meadow, Nurse

- Phillip Chavez McClarn, Survivor

- Layne Pullum, Dispatch Operator

- Freddie Rich, EMS Technician

- Bucky Rowland, Family Member

- Patsy Cross Smotherman, Nurse Technician

- Tony Sowell, Funeral Director

- Mark Wynn, Reporter & Photographer

Contents

Introduction

I recently visited the Maury County Archives building on East 6th Street in downtown Columbia, TN where over 40 years ago, this dreadful tragedy occurred. My reason for visiting had nothing to do with writing a book about the event, however, as soon as I walked through the door, I knew that this had to be my next project. It was almost as if the memories of that event were calling out to me, asking for their story to be told.

Because of that, my primary objective in this writing is to tell the story and preserve the memory of the ones who perished, while also providing answers to the disturbing questions that still persists regarding what happened that day. The worst jail fire in the history of Tennessee occurred here, in our town. It remains today, the 2nd worst jail fire in our nation's history.

News accounts were at best confusing and in many instances, they were misleading on what occurred. In the rush to get the story out, and meet deadlines, news reporters don't always have time to ensure the exactness of what is reported. They do their best, however, they depend on what witnesses say they saw, or what they think occurred, when many times our brains have a difficult time processing traumatic events. This can impact memory recall and is the primary reason that two or more can witness the same event, but, disagree on what occurred.

Additionally, there were then, and are now, people who look only for the negative. They search for people to blame and for ways to sensationalize events to intentionally create discord and ill will. Many times twisting the story into something that doesn't even resemble fact or truth. The assassination of JFK is a prime example. Somewhere in the midst of the vicious rumors, he-said, she-said stories, and numerous conspiracy theories, is the truth of what actually occurred.

My most earnest desire as I extensively researched this event has been to find that truth. We need to understand what really occurred because understanding is the first step towards true healing. This writing does not propose as truth any "he-said, she-said" statements, however, it does include eye-witness accounts of what occurred. Some of those accounts were extracted from interviews given at the time, while others are from interviews facilitated either in person, or by telephone, over the course of the past year.

Also, it's up to us to ensure that this event isn't forgotten once our generation has passed on. If such a thing were to occur, that in-and-of-itself would be yet another tragedy.

It's my understanding that some in our community blame the rescue workers for not saving everyone, but to those people, I pray that you read the following pages with an open mind and attempt to envision the situation as it unfolded.

Within this writing, I will not make accusations. I also will not be presenting a pretty picture of something that was anything but pretty. In fact, if possible, I would physically turn back the hands of time and completely eliminate the date from our history, however, the truth is that an immeasurable tragedy struck our town, leaving deep, penetrating wounds. The pain was real. The pain was intense. The pain remains with us still.

The date was Sunday, June 26, 1977. It was a hot 90-degrees and most of the residents of the small town of Columbia, TN were taking part in church functions, spending the day with family, hanging out at the pool, or taking a pleasant afternoon nap.

At the local jail, it was a day comparable to any other Sunday. Some inmates were playing cards, some were writing letters, while others were in the visitor area spending time with family.

Little did anyone know that our town was mere moments from an epic disaster. A disaster that would leave its weighty mark on every member of this community, for years to come. The worst jail fire in the history of Tennessee, both then and now.

People would soon lose their lives as toxic, choking plumes of relentless, dense, smoke would engulf the Maury County Jail just five minutes before visiting hour was to end.

There were reportedly 53 people incarcerated in the jail when a fire was set in a padded cell. The Columbia Fire Department recorded the time of the call as 1:55 PM.

I was 17-years old at the time, and remember it very well, as all residents of Maury County entered into a period of shock, disbelief, agony, and inconsolable mourning. Many people still don't care to talk about it because it is just too painful, but, this tragedy did occur, and will forever be a part of our history.

I recall when I first heard about the fire and all the confusion over what was being reported on the news, radio, television and on the streets. There were vicious rumors, as well as many legitimate questions. People wanted to understand how such a thing could happen. We all wanted to understand how one very troubled teenage boy, who was not even a part of this community, would in a matter of moments alter our lives. A boy who knew none of the victims, nor had any grievances with them. Why then did this tragedy occur? Why in our town?

It's difficult to fully comprehend how a relatively small fire could cause such destruction, however, it did, and it did so with unrelenting force and speed. Hindsight is 20/20, and we could fixate on "what if" scenarios that would benefit no one. That certainly will not bring back those who were lost. **It is time now to remember and honor the loved ones we lost.**

> *The Living owe it to those who no longer have a voice, to tell their story.*

What Happened?

It happened so very quickly, yet, the memories of that day have lingered for decades. For those who were there, the event plays over-and-over in their mind, sometimes in slow-motion where they can still see each freeze-frame moment just as it occurred. For loved ones who were not there, their vision of what occurred plays over-and over, haunting their dreams both day and night.

This entire story is almost inconceivable as it reads more like a Hollywood movie script than a real-life event. The date was June 26, 1977. The location was Columbia, TN, a small town less than an hour south of Nashville.

The Maury County Jail was a 14-year old facility standing at 201 E. 6th Street, Columbia, TN. The majority of the inmates being held in the jail at the time had not yet faced trial or been convicted of any crimes. Some of those imprisoned could've been released upon the payment of a relatively small fine.

As you might expect, multiple factors were involved leading up to the tragic event, however, before we dig in, I ask that as you read, you consider that regardless of who did, or did not do what, lives were lost. Families were destroyed, and it will benefit no one to argue about what cannot be changed.

It was a beautiful Sunday afternoon and numerous visitors had arrived at the jail to spend time with incarcerated family members.

Inside the facility were reportedly 53 inmates, 50 males, and 3 females. In addition to the inmates, there were 39 visitors, 2 deputies, 1 criminal investigator, 1 dispatcher, and 1 jailer, for a total of 97.

According to Dispatcher Layne Pullum, Jailer Cummins was responsible for the visitation area that day. Visitors who had arrived by 12:55 PM for the 1 PM visitation were processed for visitation and the inmates they were there to see were brought into the main visitation area.

Visitors were then allowed to enter the 7' wide corridor where a metal screen separated the inmates from the visitors. The screen allowed inmates and visitors to see each other, from about the shoulders up, and communicate.

There were some exceptions to the location of inmates with visitors. Such was the case for Ira (Lanny) Bellanfant, Janice Golden, and Buck Rowland.

Prisoners who had more serious charges were not housed in the workhouse area but were confined in other areas. Also, females, and juveniles, were separated from the primary jail population.

The family member visiting Lanny Bellanfant was the only visitor behind a locked door. This differs from the belief of some who say that the visitors there to see Buck Rowland were locked in, however, the evidence tells a different story.

The cell where Rowland was housed was designed for one prisoner and had double locks on the door. Outside that cell was a narrow hallway where firefighters later found two of the five visitors for Rowland. The names of the one male, and one female victim found in that small hallway were not known. The location of the other family members there visiting Rowland is also unknown.

Golden family members were standing in the corridor outside of the women's cell where Janice Golden was incarcerated. The body of one male was found in that small hallway. Some other members of the Golden family were found in the Laundry room.

The diagram below indicates the location of the inmates, their visitors, and the escape paths.

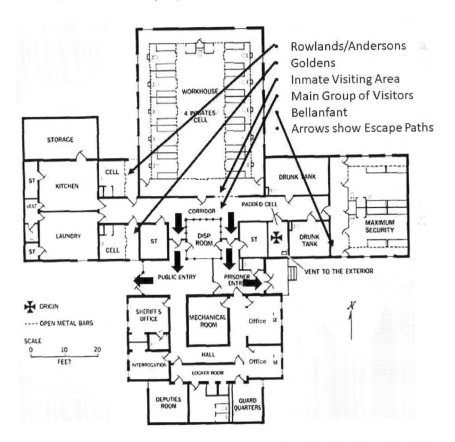

The majority of the other inmates remained locked inside their cells, or in the workhouse area, however, there were two jail trustees who were located with the visitors.

Once inside the jail facility, all who entered would be able to clearly see the rules regarding visitation posted on a large sign that was hung securely on the lobby wall.

VISITING HOURS

1 PM – 2 PM, SUNDAYS ONLY
IMMEDIATE FAMILY ONLY

NO CHILDREN UNDER 12 YEARS OF AGE WILL BE ALLOWED BEYOND THIS DOOR

THESE ARE THE ONLY ITEMS ALLOWED:
CIGARETTES

Sheriff

Just prior to 1:55 PM, a fire was intentionally set in a padded-cell occupied by a troubled teenager, who had recently run away from a rehabilitation center in Dousman, Wisconsin.

Early on during the criminal investigation, then 16-year-old Andrew (Andy) Zinmer, admitted that he intentionally set a fire, by means of a cigarette that was passed to him by a man in the corridor, who was there visiting another prisoner.

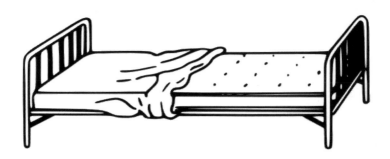

Jail Trustee Ricky Gillespie had just said goodbye to his family members, who exited the visitation area through the door on the west side of the dispatch office, when he spotted smoke creeping out from underneath the padded-cell door. Gillespie ran to the front to inform the officers on-duty and then went to grab a fire extinguisher.

Simultaneously, the teenager inside the padded cell started screaming "I'm on fire!" On-duty Jailer, Willie Cummins had already grabbed the ring of brass keys as Chief Deputy Bob Farmer, and off-duty Deputy William Earl Duke rushed to the padded cell.

As they reached the cell, Cummins unlocked the solid steel cell door and Farmer, having difficulty opening the door, placed his foot against the wall to provide enough support to force the door open.

As soon as that padded-cell door was opened a huge plume of fire, described by some at the time, as much like that from a blow torch, followed by thick, black smoke exploded into the main corridor. The blast of flames dissipated quickly, however, it was so forceful, and the heat so intense, in a matter of only seconds, it had caused significant damage to the suspended ceiling, ductwork, wiring, lighting, and equipment in the corridor and the dispatch area.

Almost instantaneously, a tremendous amount of dark, black, toxic, smoke began racing through the air-ventilation system where within a matter of moments, it had engulfed the facility.

Cummins had unlocked the cell door and then stepped back out of the way so that Farmer could open the cell. Criminal Investigator Jerry Wayne Dickey had run into the corridor and was standing near Cummins as the padded cell was opened. When he saw the flames and smoke shoot out atop the heads of Farmer and Duke he instinctively grabbed the ring of brass cell keys from Jailer Cummins, who was partially disabled with a lame leg.

Just as Farmer and Duke dragged Zinmer from the cell and out through the east exit of the facility, Dickey yelled telling the visitors to get out. Those 30 visitors were all standing with Dickey in a small area of the 7' wide corridor. The smoke was rapidly filling the corridor as many screaming visitors, dashed towards the exit at the same time. Dickey's 4-years in the US Navy had trained him to drop to the floor in the event of fire and smoke, and that is exactly what he did.

As Dickey was crushed against the wall, the keys were kicked from his hand and for a time, were lost to the tremendous soot and smoky darkness. Dickey yelled for the prisoners to drop to the floor. By this point, there was very little breathable air underneath the impenetrable smoke cloud.

According to Layne Pullum, the Dispatch on-duty, the building itself was very dimly lit. Add to that, an inordinate amount of deep, black, soot-filled smoke, and no lighting in the corridor, it was just impossible to see. Pullum said, "You literally could not see your hand in front of your face."

The facility was not equipped with an emergency backup lighting system, sprinkler system, automatic locks, or any of the safety features that are standard in penal facilities today.

The smoke was so thick, even with the keys, identifying which key went to which cell would've been extremely challenging as each key had the corresponding cell number etched into the brass, and the visibility inside the jail had plummeted to zero.

Shown next is a photo of the damage caused in the corridor by that explosion from the padded cell.

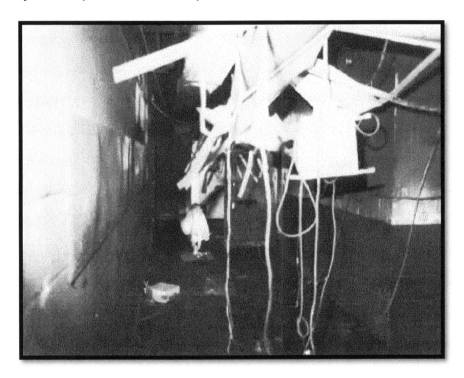

The majority of the victims were prisoners who were trapped behind locked doors, while others were visitors. One visitor was locked inside the small hallway outside the maximum security area. Eight other visitors were not locked in, but were none-the-less trapped by the thick smoke that was causing, even those who knew the facility well, to be unable to locate the exit.

The "missing" keys remain an issue of genuine contention that is a profoundly sore point for many Maury County residents. I asked the question of the keys to most who were interviewed for this book, as reports at the time, said there should've been a spare set of keys in the facility. I learned that the spare set of keys was kept in the Sheriff's office, and with Sheriff Bill Voss being out of town, his office door would've been locked.

There were news reports at the time where it was stated that only two doors would've had to have been unlocked to get everyone out, however, that statement is proven false based on the evidence of where the prisoners were found. Rowland in an individual cell, three females were in the women's cell, many were in the workhouse, the maximum security cell, and other cells within the main cell block.

Please understand that I have no intention of attempting to justify anything, nor will I condemn my fellow man. I was not there, however, based on simple logic, I will say that when that huge plume of dense smoke came charging through the jail, the lights went out, and people started yelling "fire", that would've created a scene of absolute panic and **chaos!** The word chaos is defined as complete disorder and confusion. Synonyms are mayhem, pandemonium, upheaval, uproar, commotion, disruption, free-for-all, and all-hell-breaking loose.

> **When chaos ensues, all sense of normalcy quickly disappears.**

Calvin Golden was a jail trustee at the time. As a jail trustee, Golden would have been very familiar with the layout of the building. He and his family members were in the corridor outside of a locked cell where his wife Janice was being held. That cell was only a few feet from the unlocked door on the west side of the dispatch office. That door led into the lobby and an exterior exit, yet, the dense smoke, and absolute darkness must've been completely disorienting. So much so that some members of the Golden family ended up going in the wrong direction, and perished inside the laundry room.

The Rowlands and Andersons were also standing just a few feet from the west side exit, however, they were trapped as well in the utter darkness and unable to escape.

Outside of the facility, James Duke, brother of Deputy William Earl Duke was in the back parking lot. He reported at the time that he heard a loud "woofing" sound, just as a large plume of smoke erupted from the top of the building.

That's when he heard people screaming. As he ran toward the west side exit of the jail, he saw numerous people rushing out the jail door, screaming, as a huge cloud of thick, black smoke chased immediately behind them.

According to Duke, some of them were fainting and falling backward, while in the distance he could already hear the sound of sirens from the fire dept. located only one block away. Duke instinctively ran to the door to help, but was forced back by the intensely, thick, soot-filled smoke.

> **Duke said "I ended up having to lay on the ground and hold the door open with my foot. The smoke was so heavy."**

Meanwhile, first responders were arriving and two firefighters were instructed to search for the keys, while others worked on extinguishing the fire. A medical triage unit was quickly set up and initially manned by EMS worker Freddie Rich.

Dickey crawled and felt along the side of the wall to find the way to the exit, as firefighters made their way inside.

Firefighters crawled through on their hands and knees, feeling the walls to guide them through the immense darkness. Some firefighters were sent up on the roof to the exterior vent of the padded cell where they forced water into the padded cell.

The fire itself was extinguished fairly quickly, however, the thick, deadly smoke was an entirely different matter.

Quickly the task outside turned to breaking through the exterior walls in an attempt to both get the smoke out of the jail and reach the ones who remained trapped inside. Officers and others wielded sledgehammers in attempts to knock a hole through the reinforced concrete wall in the east end at the maximum security cell.

With communication systems down, Dickey used a walkie-talkie to request the City dispatcher send a backhoe however, there was a delay, so Dickey sent someone to the city garage, less than a block away, to cut the lock off the gate and get a backhoe that they could use to knock holes in the wall.

The following diagram shows the locations on the east side at the maximum security cell, and on the west side at the main cell block where large holes were knocked into the exterior walls.

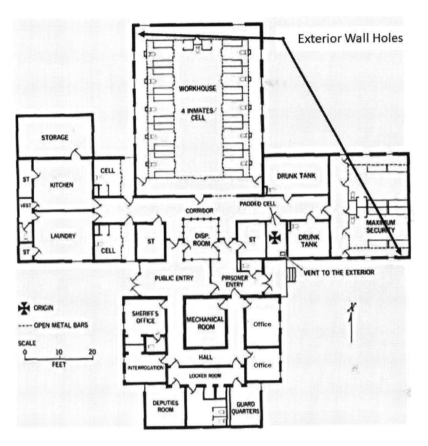

Malcolm E. Gray, Jr. (Junior), of Gray's Wrecker Service and Toodlum Haywood of Haywood's Wrecker Service, had both responded to the call for help. Each of the locked, off-duty Sheriff Dept. vehicles that were in the parking lot had to be towed out of the way so that the rescue workers would be granted clear access to the jail, and have room to set up a triage unit.

The wrecker operators further assisted officers by running a cable from a truck through one of the holes that was opened up on the corner of the building. The tow cable was wrapped tightly around the bars of the cells inside where a number of the inmates were trapped. The bars were snatched off by the truck so that access could be gained to those prisoners.

Below a wrecker is seen working to snatch bars out of the jail.

Similar efforts were made to snatch the bars off of the exterior windows. That proved more challenging as the wrecker was seen with both front wheels lifted into the air while the truck strained against iron bars extending deep into the concrete-block walls. The structure was built to keep people in, and it was holding true to its design.

Phil Wright, a foreman from a local steel plant was there with his sledgehammer assisting in the effort of smashing through exterior walls. He offered the following comment, "We finally broke through the wall and found our way into a cellblock where we knocked open a door. There were four men in there and about six in the cell next door. **Nobody could've gotten out of there. The smoke almost got me too.**"

There were so many others who answered the call. Civil Defense workers J.C. Inman, Clayton Barnes, and Jimmy

Scott, and many others rushed to help as soon as they heard of the fire.

Clayton Barnes had been at home when the fire broke out and his young teenage daughter was talking to a friend on their home telephone when the operator broke in on the call with an urgent call for Barnes. He quickly rushed to the jail to help.

When medical professionals arrived from the Maury County Hospital, they relieved the EMS technicians and assumed responsibility of the medical triage area, so the EMS teams could begin transporting patients to the local hospital.

Shown above is a photograph of the large crowd that had gathered in the street. Police officers can be seen, and many of those in the street beleived they were there to shoot any inmates who might attempt to escape, however, that was not the case. Their primary role was to keep the peace, and not allow the horrible situation to grow worse than it already was.

Out of the 75 who were transported to the hospital, only one suffered actual burns. That individual was Andy Zinmer, the troubled young man who had intentionally set the fire altering so many lives. Five were treated and released, twelve were transferred to other facilities, and sixteen were admitted. Of those being treated at the local hospital, six were visitors and six were firefighters.

Pictured next are some of the first responder vehicles that arrived on the scene.

This horrific, and unimaginable event, occurred in a day long before cell phones were readily available. News traveled via radio stations, television, and word of mouth, and for the local community, mass confusion ruled the day, even regarding what was being reported via the radio stations, and later by the newspapers.

With emotions overwrought, it is no wonder that the subject remains taboo today. So many lives were transformed that day, all the result of one senseless, and painful act, made by a clearly troubled individual.

Rumors, falsehoods, and half-truths quickly filled the streets creating an unsettled environment where no one knew who, or what, to believe.

Less than 30-hours after the incarceration of the 16-year old Andy Zinmer, heavy equipment, and sledgehammers were used to break through the thick concrete block jail walls, in an effort to provide any means of escape to those trapped inside.

Once the keys were located, firefighters wearing gas masks struggled through the still dense, toxic, smoke. Crawling on their hands and knees, using only the walls to guide them to reach victims cells where they worked to match keys with locks.

Most of the victims were found in a corner of the workhouse area. Each person within the facility was completely drenched in deep, dark, black soot.

There are numerous stories. Some of intentional wrongdoing, errors, and others of true heroism. The last sounds many of the lost may have heard would have been those of rescuers, in valiant efforts, trying to reach them.

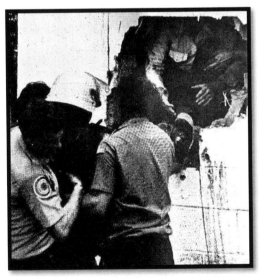

The heat must've been agonizing for the firefighters in their protective suits and headgear. It was 90-degrees outside. I can only imagine what it would've been inside that jail, where there was nothing but heat, smoke, and utter darkness.

Pictured above is Firefighter Ben Frierson being assisted out of the facility after he was overcome with smoke.

To the crowd standing in the street it appeared as if all of the victims were black, however, that was because every person being removed from the facility was covered with dark, black soot leaving their race indistinguishable.

In truth, when looking at the ethnicity of the 42 who lost their lives that day, there were 27 white lives lost, with 8 of those being visitors, and 15 black lives lost, with 1 being a visitor.

Each of the visitors who had been inside the main visitor area of the corridor escaped, however, the 9 visitors who had been located just a few feet away, did not. Of the 53 incarcerated at the time, 33 perished, and 20 survived. This was a traumatic event of epic proportion for all.

Shown next is one of many parking lot scenes.

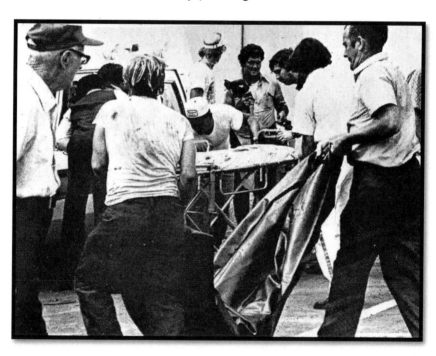

Victims were transported to the local hospital, as ambulances raced in from the surrounding counties. Twelve ambulances and hearses from four local funeral homes transported victims to the Maury County Hospital where the twenty-day old ER (emergency room) was put to the test. A temporary morgue was set up inside the unfinished physical-therapy room, in a wing of the facility that was still under construction. Luckily, the patients began arriving during a shift change so double the typical staff was there at the time. Pictured below is the Maury County Hospital.

Hospital Administrator William R. Walter quickly put into action their well-rehearsed emergency preparedness plan, which included a coded phrase that off-duty staff members would be able to decipher.

Local radio stations were instructed to begin broadcasting that coded message "a yellow pearl has been found." To the off-duty staff, the phrase was an urgent call to report in, and meant, "a disaster of the worst order."

Phone calls were also made to off-duty personnel. One such call was received by Stephanie Belt. She and her fiancé Eddie Allred were preparing to attend an event associated with their upcoming wedding scheduled for the following Saturday. The call came in with only one question asked. "Can you report in?" The caller did not even wait for an answer. None was required. Stephanie and Eddie both immediately headed to the hospital.

Doctors and nurses came from all around the mid-state area to assist. The Farm Commune in Summertown sent a doctor, three nurses, and a medical technician to assist.

Because there was so much soot, the face of each victim who perished that day was wiped clean by a nurse, so that family members would be able to identify them. All forms of personal identification, such as a driver's license, remained inside the jail.

The following days, weeks, and months were indeed somber as funerals were conducted and loved ones reluctantly said their goodbyes. It seemed as though there was a cloud over the entire community. A cloud of absolute despair and grief.

> **By 3:30 PM the jail stood void of prisoners, virtually empty with nothing but memories of tragedy. All of the victims were out. Either of their own accord or by the aid of rescue workers.**

Once all of the weapons were removed from the facility, the operations of the Sheriff's Department physically relocated to the Columbia City Police Department.

This horror occurred while Sheriff Bill Voss was out of town. He was not aware of the jail fire until on his way home from a convention in Memphis, he stopped for a late lunch and heard people talking about the jail fire in Maury County. I can only imagine what went through his mind as he returned to the facility and saw the utter devastation.

Voss had never anticipated anything of this nature occurring in the facility that he, and others, considered fireproof. The county for years had an old, two-story jail that previously stood on that very spot. That facility had been torn down and replaced by the more modern building in 1963-64.

The once new block and steel jail now stood desolate. With black soot stains at each opening and large, gaping holes in the once solid, exterior walls.

The deadly agent claiming the lives of so many that day was not fire. Dr. George Mayfield, the county medical examiner stated that he sent blood samples from ten of the victims to a highly respected national laboratory.

He reported that "Results of the tests show all of the victims had lethal levels of carbon monoxide." According to Mayfield, "carbon monoxide is one of the most lethal gases known and almost all fire victims have lethal concentrations of carbon monoxide in their blood at the time of death."

When researching the effects of extremely high doses of carbon monoxide I found that it can cause unconsciousness after only 2–3 breaths, and death in less than three minutes.

Multiple black, sooty finger marks, as shown next, would've been visible to Voss as he viewed the damaged facility which only a day before had stood as the 18th safest jail in the state of Tennessee.

Contrary to many of the false statements that were made at the time. Not one person burned to death in this fire. In fact, Zinmer was the only person who suffered any burns at all, and he survived.

The following photos were included with the inspection report from the National Fire Protection Association (NFPA). Shown below is one of the large holes knocked into the exterior wall. Notice the bars that were snatched off by wrecker operators.

Shown next is the jail exterior at the west-side parking area.

State of TN Official Report

The State of TN Fire Protection Division conducted official investigations and an extensive report was compiled by Tom D. Copeland, Chief of Fire Protection and Sr. Fire Protection Specialist, Wm. M. Steffenhagen.

Much of the report focuses on the technicalities of how the fire spread and the combustible materials that released the deadly toxins, while other report sections addressed the structural design and layout of the facility.

I will share some of the less technical information contained in the original report.

"The Maury County Jail and Sheriff's office was constructed in 1963-64 of basically fire-resistive construction. The walls and partitions for this one-story penal and office facility were of concrete masonry units supporting a concrete channel slab.

"The original building was 7,200 square feet in floor area with a later addition of a storage room to the kitchen and a non-communicating garage along the northeast portion of the building

"The dispatcher's office afforded visual surveillance of the corridors and personnel movement through the wired glass view panels.

"Portable fire extinguishers were provided. There was no fire alarm system, automatic extinguishing system, or emergency lighting.

"The fire, which produced large quantities of thick smoke resulted in the death of 42 individuals and the injury of 29 others. Of the fatalities, 33 were prisoners and 9 were visitors.

"Investigations indicate that jail personnel in the dispatcher's office were alerted to the fire. They proceeded to the padded cell and opened the cell door to remove the prisoner. When the cell door was opened, smoke and heat knocked the officers to the floor. The officers were able to remove the prisoner from the cell.

"The facility quickly filled with smoke, and the visitors were directed to leave. In the ensuing confusion, the jail keys were lost for a period of time.

"The fire department received an alarm at 1:55 p.m. and responded from their main station located about two blocks away. As the firefighters arrived, black smoke was reported coming out of the building. Firefighters began rescue and extinguishing operations by breaching the jail walls and roof with the aid of wrecker operators and volunteers.

"Extinguishment of the fire was by hose lines advanced down the corridor and a hose stream directed from the roof into the roof vent of the padded cell."

"Smoke and soot accumulations were extensive throughout the building. Except for the office area, the smoke appeared to have traveled primarily through the corridors and out the east and west exit doors and the windows in the small cells near the service areas. Smoke staining was noted on the outside of the building at these windows and doors.

"The fire in the padded cell appeared to have consumed about 80% of the foam padding, almost all of the covering material, and a small percentage of the wood backing. No other combustibles except clothing and perhaps a blanket were reported to have been in the cell.

"All of the padding on the door and north wall was burned away and the wood heavily charred. The wood was burned away along the top of the door and near the floor in the northwest corner of the room. The individual panels appeared to have burned relatively uniformly from top to bottom. However, the burn depth varied from the north to the south end of the room.

"The panels on the north end of the room had all of the foam consumed. The panels on the south end of the room had about half of the foam depth burned away. No significant amount of combustibles outside of the padded cell was involved. A small amount of concrete appeared to have **spalled** on a beam in the padded cell and exposed steel-reinforcing material. The aluminum grille for the light fixture in the padded cell melted slightly at one corner.

> *Spalled: Fire can cause mechanical stress and chemical changes inside the structural concrete, which may decrease mechanical properties such as strength or the modulus of elasticity. This can cause steam pressure, leading to cracking of the concrete, known as spalling or temperature shock.*

"Apparently the fire plume extended into the corridor through the open cell door and caused heat damage to the suspended ceiling, ductwork, wiring, lighting, and other equipment in the corridor. The suspended ceiling was damaged and dislodged to about the dispatcher's office.

The next two photographs show the door leading into the padded cell, and looking inside the cell.

"Smoke spread in the cell areas primarily through openings and cracks and secondarily by the heating/air conditioning system. However, the filters in the mechanical units were heavily loaded with soot. The supply and return air grilles in the maximum security cell area had relatively little buildup of smoke and soot. The drunk tank beside the padded cell had a pillow stuffed in the grille. The pillow was probably placed there prior to the fire to reduce airflow for comfort reasons. The supply air grilles in the remaining cells, kitchen, and laundry showed signs of having discharged smoke and soot".

Pictured below is a soot-covered bed and pillow.

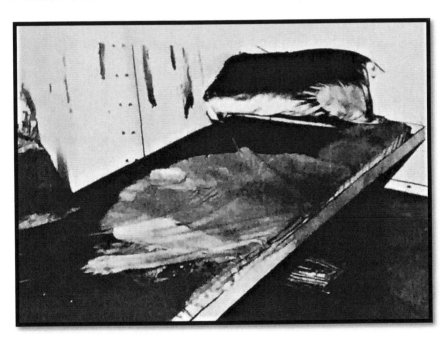

"Heavy smoke staining indicated smoke spread into the two small cells near the service areas by way of openings between the top of the corridor partition and the roof deck (above the suspended ceiling). Smoke staining in the laundry was heavy near the interface of the partition and the roof deck along the east wall. Also, the metal plumbing access door serving the cell adjoining the laundry appeared to have been ajar. There was heavy smoke staining around this opening. Smoke spread into the workhouse principally through the visitor screen.

"Smoke inhalation victims were found in the laundry, the two cells near the service area, the workhouse, and the maximum security cell area. Survivors were found in the workhouse cell area and its visitor vestibule. The occupant of the padded cell survived and was the only person who received burn injuries.

> **"This fire caused relatively little heat damage to the building. However, it points out the fact that a relatively small fire can create conditions capable of killing a large number."**

Agencies and organizations involved in the investigation included:

- City of Columbia Fire Department
- National Bureau of Standards
- National Fire Protection Association
- Society of Plastics Industry
- Tennessee Department of Safety
- Tennessee Division of Fire Prevention

The Facility

The Maury County Jail was built on the site where the old jail had been located. That building was a two-story home that had been converted into a jail with a workhouse in the rear, offices in the front, and the Sheriff's dwelling upstairs. Shown below is the old facility that was used from 1886 until 1962.

In 1963 that structure was torn down and replaced with a one-story, fire-resistive jail that was modern for its day. A 7200 sq. ft. concrete block and steel reinforced building, ranked at the time, as 18th in safety out of 102 jails located in the state.

The building was not equipped with sprinklers. In 1977 they were not a required safety feature. The facility was also not equipped with automatic locking/unlocking doors. Each door required its own individual key. Below is a diagram of the 1963 jail floor plan.

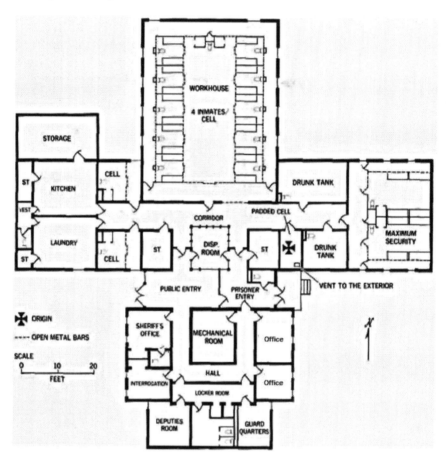

The jail had passed a fire inspection just ten days prior to that disastrous event. The inspection was conducted by Columbia Fire Inspector Wayne Hickman, who reported that the facility met all of the national fire code regulations for jails. The only shortcoming noted was regarding not having printed handouts of jail rules and regulations for the inmates. A minor infraction.

The Sheriff's office and other administrative offices were in the front section of the building and the workhouse, or main part of the jail area was in the center. The workhouse had a large open space with tables in the middle and cells located around the perimeter. There was an opening in the wall covered by a thick, heavy, metal screen where inmates were able to speak with their visitors.

The dispatcher's office sat between two metal doors providing access to the long corridor outside the workhouse area. To the left were cells for females, and other inmates that needed to be separated from the main population. To the right were the main evidence room, the padded cell, two drunk tanks, and a maximum security wing.

The padded cell was 6' x 10' with a 10' tall ceiling. Serving as the ceiling was the concrete channel roof. The cell floor was painted concrete, and the concrete masonry walls had padded material panels approximately 6' tall, attached to steel angles.

The metal cell door was padded on the interior and contained a "bean hole" food tray where food could be passed through. In addition, there was an 8" x 4" supply air grille over the doorway and a gravity vent in the Southeast corner of the ceiling.

The padded cell material itself reportedly was foam rubber covered by Herculite 80 which is made of polyvinyl chloride (PVC) that was initially believed to be fire-resistant. Tom Copeland, Chief of the Fire Protection Division at the State Fire Marshal's office, said at the time that PVC was being scrutinized as a possible cancer-causing agent.

Joseph Nowinski, Vice President of Herculite said, at the time, that the company is investigating where the material came from and admitted that the company does circulate a product flyer which clearly states its materials are flameproof and will not support combustion. However, according to Nowinski, "fireproof and flameproof do not mean the same thing. Our material will not support a flame, but it will melt. And it doesn't emit cyanide."

> **Various reports, however, did list cyanide, a toxic gas that doesn't allow the blood to receive oxygen, as the cause of some of the deaths.**

State Fire Marshal Eugene Hartsook reported that test results from the Tennessee Crime Laboratory confirmed the cell was padded with polyurethane, a highly flammable foam rubber, and copolymer, a mixture of butadiene and styrene. He also reported that blood tests they had conducted on eight of the victims showed three of the eight died of Cyanide poisoning, and five from carbon monoxide.

When the jail was built in 1963-64, the padded cell was lined with a copolymer padding, and since that time, replacement panels made of polyurethane were used.

Tom Oat, the news editor of the Norge Connecticut Bulletin, a newspaper that had previously conducted a very extensive national survey looking into such fires, described cyanide as a flash-type of gas with great heat intensity. Oat said, "If the padding inside that cell was made of a polyfoam material or a petroleum-based polyurethane, as many as 1200 different gases, including cyanide, could've been emitted.

Oat went on to say, "We conducted a test in an open field using a 3-inch, regular polyurethane mattress." The following photo is from a similar type of test. The dark, black, plume of smoke, already at the ceiling, is evident.

"We burned it and it was totally consumed in three minutes with thick, billowing, black smoke reaching over 30 feet above and 15 feet wide. We could not see anything through the smoke."

The 4" thick padding in the 6' x 10' padded cell covered all four walls and the door. TFPA reported that 80% of the foam padding was consumed during the fire, along with almost all of the covering material.

Subsequent to the fire, the City Fire Marshal provided a list of numerous recommendations for the jail that went beyond the

1977 fire-safety regulations. His recommendations included the complete removal of that padded cell, the addition of an electronic locking/unlocking system for jail cells, a sprinkler system, smoke detectors, and making the visitor area remote from where it was previously located.

This tragedy sheds light on the need, particularly in this type of facility, for organization and genuine preparedness. I now understand why as children in school, we were all constantly participating in fire-drills and tornado-drills. All so that if such an event were to occur, we would know what to do.

> **I will never forget driving past the jail days after the fire and seeing the gaping holes, surrounded with black soot, in the concrete block walls, the darkened windows, and debris out on the sidewalk. It was a foreboding sight to behold. A sight that I will never forget.**

The most extensive structural damage to the jail was within the padded cell itself. Outside the cell, heat, smoke and dark soot damaged ceiling tiles, ductwork, wiring, plumbing, and lighting in the corridor and the dispatch area. However, apart from that, all other damage had been caused intentionally by rescue-worker efforts to save those who were inside.

Because the structural damage was relatively minimal, the decision was eventually reached to rebuild the facility, as it was, but without the padded cell. That jail reopened on Oct. 17, 1977, and served Maury County for the following 22 years.

Shown next is Sheriff Bill Voss standing outside one of the newly renovated cells. The facility was rebuilt to match the earlier design, however, without the padded cell.

That building was replaced with the facility below in 1999.

According to **Enoch George** who was sheriff during the 1999 jail transition, inmates were transferred to the new facility on Feb. 12, 1999. Just after that transition was complete, **Tim Carter**, a member of the Sheriff's Maintenance Department captured the following photographs of the jail interior.

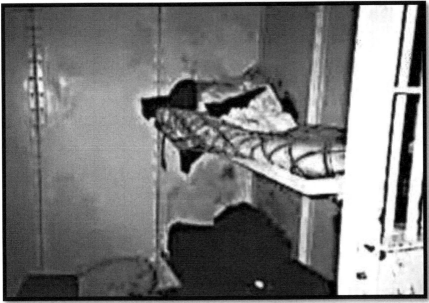

It's evident that the years had taken their toll on the facilty.

The building was eventually remodeled and is today the home of the Maury County Archives. A location where I was spent many long hours gathering much of the information used to compile this writing.

Below is a photograph of the Archives building as it looks today.

The Teen Who Set the Fire

According to Wisconsin police records, Andy Zinmer was first arrested on Feb. 28, 1975, at the age of 14, and charged with igniting a fire on a towel rack in a building in Superior, WI. Authorities there said that Zinmer had also been questioned the previous June after he reportedly threatened to set fire to his own home.

Zinmer grew up in a home with his mother and four siblings. His father left when Zinmer was 11, and his younger brother had mental issues requiring constant care. Zinmer's mother was quoted at the time as saying, "Andy was a quiet child and was never demanding. When he was four-years old he fell down a flight of stairs and lay unconscious for several minutes.

"There was no evidence of brain damage, but, years later, tests indicated abnormalities. Andy was so excited when he was led off by his older sister, for his first day of school. He had been anticipating school for a long time, but, school became a scene of disappointments and humiliations. Slow at learning to read, often preoccupied and unable to concentrate, he failed the first grade and had to repeat it.

"By the 6th grade his problems had become severe enough that psychiatrist counsel was sought. After testing, Andy was placed in special classes for children.

"About five weeks before the jail fire, he was taken to a home for disturbed boys. There he quickly faced the same kinds of problems. He was teased, and a boy his age split his lip in a fight, giving him a wound that required several stitches."

After the 1977 jail fire, Zinmer was taken by helicopter to a Nashville hospital where he was treated for both 2nd and 3rd-degree burns on 25% of his body. He was later transported back to the Maury County hospital for continued medical care.

Upon his initial arrest in Maury County, Zinmer was placed in the only juvenile cell at the Maury County jail, however, he was moved into the padded cell after he intentionally flooded the juvenile unit by causing a toilet to overflow. With him being a juvenile, the padded cell was the only option for him to be separated from the adult inmates.

That Sunday afternoon Zinmer called out to a visitor who was in the corridor outside his cell and asked for a cigarette. The visitor who was not acquainted with Zinmer reportedly handed him one lit cigarette and one unlit cigarette. Both were passed through the small food tray in the padded cell door.

Zinmer then went to work. It is said that in addition to the two cigarettes, he had a leftover candy-bar wrapper. He may have used that wrapper, and possibly an article of clothing, to ignite the fire.

Described as an emotionally disturbed loner by his mother, Zinmer had escaped from a treatment center for emotionally troubled teenagers 38 miles west of Milwaukee, WI just three days prior to this event.

The Maury County Sheriff's Department received a dispatch report of a hitchhiker on I-65 around midnight on Friday, June 24th. Deputies were able to locate the 5' 11", 211-pound male at approximately 12:30 AM on Saturday, June 25th. The boy readily admitted to being a runaway from Wisconsin.

While Zinmer was being treated at the Vanderbilt Hospital in Nashville, the Tennessean newspaper reported that while in the intensive care unit, witnesses said Zinmer was "giving the nurses a hard time. **"He kept asking for a cigarette in the oxygen-filled intensive care unit, and nurses kept telling him no smoking is allowed."**

As a lengthy court battle ensued, Zinmer was represented by Nashville Attorney **Lionel Barrett**, who stated that he would not object to a psychiatric evaluation, but would object to his client being tried as an adult.

District Attorney Robert Gay was absolutely relentless filing charges of arson, and 42 counts of manslaughter in Juvenile Court, however, those charges proved unsuccessful. **Chief Deputy Bob Farmer** then signed a petition, still in juvenile court, charging Zinmer with 42 counts of 2nd-degree murder. Staff in the District Attorney's office said at the time that a 2nd-degree murder charge indicates a "grossly reckless and illegal act which results from implied malice toward the human beings that lost their lives."

Gay was successful in charging Zinmer as an adult and taking the matter out of the juvenile court system. As the trial against

Zinmer progressed **Farmer testified that moments after he and Duke dragged Zinmer from the burning padded cell at the jail, he said, "I did it. I started the fire."**

Shown below is Sheriff Voss, and others, escorting Zinmer to one of many court appearances.

Zinmer had a few altercations while imprisoned at the Maury County Jail as many of the inmates wanted to "rough him up" because of the fire. Some were successful, and one night he was treated at the local hospital for injuries inflicted by upset inmates.

Ultimately Zinmer did plead guilty to 42 counts of involuntary manslaughter, and one count of arson. Readily admitting that he set the fire, however, stating he had no intention of causing anyone harm. He spent 18-months imprisoned in Tennessee and was transported back to Superior, WI where he would serve out the probation.

Since that time he reportedly has had only minor scrapes with the law, however, with 2nd and 3rd-degree burns covering over 25% of his body, he will forevermore carry the physical scars of his actions that day. Just as this community continues to carry deep-set emotional scars.

Memories of Survivors

I recently spoke with **Phillip Chevez McClarn**, who was an inmate at the time of the jail fire. McClarn started out saying, "The whole thing was very spiritual for me. I was raised going to church every Sunday because my parents, who were good Christian people, made me go. I, however, had made some bad choices, which is why I was in jail that day. I remember it just like it was yesterday. I was asleep in my bunk when a song playing on the radio woke me up.

> **"The song playing was an old gospel hymn and the words of that song touched my heart in an amazing way. *Is there anybody hear, that loves my Jesus? Is there anybody here, that loves my Lord?* I stood up and said YES!"**

"I cried and thanked the Lord that morning. I thanked Jesus for allowing me to be there, to be alive. I felt like I was filled with the Holy Spirit. Any feelings of hate that I had previously held in my heart were gone. If anyone of those inmates had asked me for a cigarette that morning, I would've given them my entire pack. It's difficult to put the feeling into words, other than to say that it was a very spiritual feeling of pure love.

"I remember having breakfast, and then later in the day being called into the bullpen for visiting hour. I was sitting there talking to my Dad when he said, "I think I smell smoke."

"One of his friends named Ernest was the jail cook and I just made a joke about it and said it was probably Ernest burning something. Dad laughed but said, no, this isn't that kind of smell. This is more like a gas kind of smell."

About that time, they started seeing smoke and McClarn told his Dad to leave. When his Dad found the exit door locked, McClarn told him to tell the Dispatcher to open the door. The door was opened and his Father was able to leave.

McClarn told a news reporter at the time that he saw "a flame shoot all the way through the visitor screen into the workhouse cell," and it was followed by choking smoke that filled the hallway.

"Probably ten seconds later, smoke was racing down the hall and I could see two men dragging a guy out towards the east door. There was one on each side of him holding a shoulder with his feet dragging behind. Within 30 seconds the entire place was filling with thick, black smoke.

"I asked Robert Duke to get me a towel and wet it. He handed me the towel and I wrapped it around my face and head like a turban. Then I laid down at the door and just went to sleep. I never coughed or experienced any pain. I just went to sleep and woke up two-days later in St. Thomas Hospital having no idea how I got there. When I came to, I had no burns, bruises, or scratches on my body. Nothing.

"I don't know why God saved me that day, but I know that he did. My memories of that morning are beautiful because I had never felt such a strong connection to God before, and that changed my life. When I got out of jail I said that I was going to dedicate part of my life to Jesus, so I joined the Columbia United Mass Choir and years later I joined a gospel choir that traveled with the River Dance Group. One of our trips was to Dublin, Ireland where our Christian gospel group was even invited to sing in some of the Catholic churches.

"The day of the jail fire was my daughter's third birthday. I went on to have two more beautiful daughters, one of which passed away last year. I miss her, but, it was her time to go. I know that she is in heaven right now, and the physical pain she endured here is no more. Before that jail fire I used to fear death. Now I don't fear death anymore."

> **"I know a lot of people want to talk about conspiracy theories and how deputies planned the whole thing, but I can tell you that is not true. Of course, some of those folks don't want to hear me say that, but it was a freak, bad accident, and nothing more."**

Kevin Wells, from Indianapolis, Illinois was an inmate when the fire broke out. Wells was being held there while awaiting a decision from the local grand jury on a 3rd-degree burglary charge against him. He spoke to a reporter who met with him at the local hospital where he provided the following statement of what occurred.

"This dude was burning mattresses in the padded cell. We saw the smoke coming from under the door, then everybody started hollering Fire!

"We started hollering for the dispatcher to open the door, and he said he couldn't find the keys. It took way too long to get us out.

"They were hollering one man is dead! Then three more died, and I passed out.

"There were two mattresses over my face. I was lying on the floor, and I was doing a lot of praying. After I passed out, the next thing I remember, I was in the hospital here. I don't know who got me out, or how they got me out."

Jack Davis reported at the time, "It looked like a big ball of smoke rolling towards us. The smoke was so thick I could not see."

"We all crawled under our bunks looking for oxygen, said our prayers and figured all was lost. I don't know how I got out of there. The smoke kept getting thicker and thicker, you could not breathe."

Davis reported at the time that he did not know when he was pulled from the jail, or who pulled him out.

Many of the survivors have similar stories to tell. Their lives were saved by brave individuals who were there placing their own lives at risk, doing anything they could do to help to save people who they did not even know. Deputies, Firefighters, EMS workers, and so very many more.

Another survivor who had been in the workhouse was **Terry Kenney**. Kennedy said "The smoke started rolling into the area and everybody started running out of the visitor gallery.

"I could see the blaze coming down the hall. Pretty soon, everybody started looking for towels, and I grabbed a towel and wet it, and put the towel over my mouth. Then the lights went out. I got down on the floor although I would get back up thinking I heard the keys to unlock the door. I remember seeing everyone else down on the floor. I think I was one of the last to pass out."

Seymore Meyers, an inmate at the time of the fire was able to escape death by climbing into a shower and keeping the water on as long as he could. Meyers passed out and woke up in the emergency room of St. Thomas in Nashville. When interviewed, he commented that **"the smoke was so thick I couldn't see my hand in front of my face."**

Being treated for severe smoke inhalation and cuts on his head and arms, Meyers also said "I started getting wet rags and putting them over my body. People were crawling over me to get to the water. I passed wet rags to some of them. I don't know what happened to those prisoners."

William Hann was an inmate located in the workhouse at the time of the fire and was interviewed at the hospital. He said "I was sitting at a table talking to some of the other people in the area when I first noticed the smoke. I looked up, saw the smoke and heard screaming. I started gagging and I got a towel, wet it, and put it in my mouth before I went back to my bunk to lay down. People were running around in circles until they passed out." Hann went on to say a friend Lee C. Neal died near him, and he thought he was going to die too. He does not remember being pulled out of the jail or being transported to St. Thomas Hospital in Nashville.

> **David Martin was interviewed at the Maury County Hospital. Martin said "I heard somebody screaming and I saw smoke coming into the area. It was black and stuffy, and I couldn't breathe."**

He grabbed a blanket, stuck it in the commode and then placed it over his mouth, and the mouth of his cousin, Robert Jones. "I remember nothing after that, although I came to once in the helicopter."

The workhouse inmates were told to drop to the floor so they could breathe. As the smoke filled the visitor gallery, inmates covered their mouths with wet cloths. Seconds later they were passing out.

Garry Pillow, a local man who was incarcerated for a minor offense was sitting on his bunk reading at the time. Pillow said in a 1977 interview, "I heard visitors in the jail yelling fire. I got off my bunk and **saw the heavy smoke coming down the hallway**.

"Everyone in the workhouse area was lying on the floor. I got in the shower and wet myself down, but the water got turned off somehow, then I put a towel over my face, and got down on the floor and started praying. What else could I do?"

In the photo to the right, Pillow demonstrated from his hospital bed how he covered his face with a wet towel to keep from breathing in the smoke. Pillow, and many others used this type of technique to literally escape a certain sentence of death.

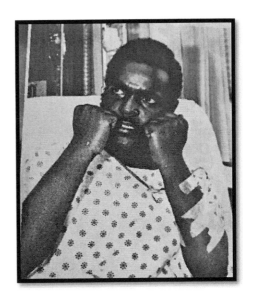

Amazingly, 20 of the 53 inmates survived that horrific event.

Memories of Sheriff's Dept. Employees

Dispatch operator Layne Pullum was on-duty that day and was located inside the dispatch office which faced into the workhouse area. In the office with him that day was the Jailer Willie Cummins.

Pullum previously held the combined role of jailer/dispatcher and when working as a jailer, he would've been responsible for bringing the inmates, who had visitors, into the visitation area. His detailed, step-by-step process is as follows: Five minutes prior to the 1 PM visitation time, he would pick up the visitor sign-in sheet  and the keys to the jail. From there he would move into the main corridor and unlock the steel door going into the inmate visitation area. As he moved into that room he would relock the door behind him, and proceed to unlock the door going into the workhouse area.

Once inside the workhouse, he would line up the prisoners who had family there to visit and move them into the inmate visitation area. Then he would unlock the door leading into the corridor, relocking it behind him as he exited the room. Many times there would be a Deputy standing at that door to ensure safety.

From there he would step into the lobby and direct the visitors into the 7' wide corridor where they would stand at the metal screen to visit with their family members.

Family members visiting inmates that were not housed in the main workhouse were allowed to stand just outside of the specific cell during the visitation. Such was the case with the Andersons, Goldens, and Rowlands. However, because of the additional security as a result of the recent jailbreak, the rumor of an intended jailbreak, and the late arrival of one visitor that day. The door between the main corridor and the maximum security cell corridor on the east end of the jail, that would typically have been unlocked, was indeed locked.

The diagram below, shows the location of visitors, and the escape paths.

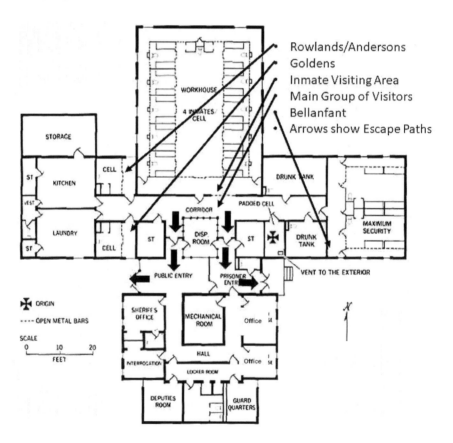

Rowlands/Andersons
Goldens
Inmate Visiting Area
Main Group of Visitors
Bellanfant
• Arrows show Escape Paths

Luther Bellanfant Jr. had arrived late that day wanting to visit with his son Lanny. **Chief Deputy Farmer**, having a son of his own, and feeling compassion for Bellanfant, acquiesced and allowed him in.

Bellanfant was inside the maximum security area, therefore, Mr. Bellanfant would've been taken into the main corridor, where he would've walked past the padded cell, and into the corridor of the maximum security cell area to visit with his son.

As the end of the visiting hour approached, the parking lot was filled with locked, off-duty deputy vehicles, and inside the jail, 30 visitors were standing inside the main corridor. It had been reported at the time that the metal doors on both sides of the dispatch office remained locked after the fire broke out, however, the evidence shows that both doors were unlocked.

Deputy William Earl Duke was not on duty that day but he

and his brother James had stopped by to wash Duke's car in the back lot, behind the jail. After finishing up on the car, Duke walked into the jail and was talking with Chief Deputy Farmer and Criminal Investigator Jerry Dickey when visitors started beating on the dispatch office window. "I remember that we rushed through the door to the left, or west side of the dispatch office, and I saw black, sooty smoke sifting from the bottom of the padded cell door. Zinmer was banging on the door and yelling.

"As that door was opened, thick black smoke was covering Zinmer. I reached in, grabbed his arms. Farmer and I then dragged him out to the east side parking lot."

Pullum said "Just prior to the visitation period ending, even though I wasn't able to see everything that was going on I could tell that a really big commotion had broken out in the corridor. Cummins jumped up to see what was happening, and joined Chief Deputy Farmer, and Deputy Duke in the corridor as the kid in the padded cell yelled "I'm on fire!"

After that padded cell door was opened, things dramatically changed. As Farmer and Duke quickly dragged Zinmer out of the building, to the east side parking area.

> **Dickey yelled telling the visitors to get out, and then turned and looked at Calvin Golden who was standing in the corridor and said, "Calvin, get your family out."**

Just as he said spoke those words, the smoke raced through the corridor and turned the jail into a scene of unimaginable horror.

Duke said, "Getting Zinmer out took only a few moments, however, by the time I got back inside, smoke had engulfed the corridor and dispatch area, and was quickly traveling into the main area of the jail. Duke said. "The smoke was thick, black soot that burned when it was inhaled. I quickly ran outside and removed a couple of shotguns from deputy vehicles in the parking area, thinking that I could create a space to hold the prisoners as they came out, however, Farmer told me that the keys were lost in the soot. I knew then that we would not be needing the shotguns.

"My brother James was laying on the ground holding the door open with his foot as I took a deep breath and crawled in to search for the keys. When I ran out of air, I turned and stood

72

but I could not see anything. I will never forget the feeling of standing there in utter darkness. **I started yelling and flailing my arms in every direction and finally I felt a vending machine that I was able to use as a directional marker pointing the way to the exit.** I was about 10' outside the facility before I could see or breathe fresh air."

Pullum recalled that the door on the east side of the dispatch area was left standing wide open. Evidence provided in the State Fire Marshal's inspection report would later confirm that the east door was indeed standing open. Rescue workers reported that they were accessing the corridor via both the east and west sides of the dispatch office.

The next thing Pullum saw was a crowd of people rushing out yelling and screaming, followed by a rush of thick, black, smoke. Pullum stated, "I heard one of the prisoners yelling, and I yelled back telling him to get a wet rag or towel and wrap it around his nose and mouth so he could breathe."

The jail dispatch area became completely dysfunctional within seconds of the explosion of fire and smoke. Because of that, Chief Deputy Farmer instructed Pullum to rush over to the City Dispatch office and help out there.

> **Chief Deputy Bob Farmer commented at the time, 'We didn't really think about the jail catching fire," Why would they, brick and steel don't burn. "We've had inmates in the past try to set fire to that padding and none were successful. I have no idea how Zinmer was able to do it."**

When asking Pullum about the padded cell itself, he described the padding cover as a material similar to Naugahyde. He also said that Sheriff Voss required frequent jail inspections that included the padded cell, so he was confident that there were no visible issues with the padding, but, he does suspect that Zinmer was able to rip a hole in the padding to start the fire.

Criminal Investigator Jerry Wayne Dickey was on duty that day and was quick to act when Zinmer began to yell that he was on fire.

Dickey typically did not work on Sundays, however, Farmer had called the night before and asked him to come in because there were rumors of an escape attempt planned for Sunday.

Chief Deputy Farmer was quoted the following day saying, "I had heard a rumor that there might be a breakout attempt on that Sunday." Since there had been a successful breakout just 3-days prior, and two of those inmates had been captured and were again inside the facility, this rumor was something that he had to take seriously.

As Dickey and I were speaking at the Maury County Archives building he mentioned that the water cooler hanging on the lobby wall is in the same location where a water cooler stood in 1977. A location that he utilized as a direction marker during his blind crawl to the east exit of the facility.

While rescue workers and others were inside bringing victims out, **Duke** and his brother were in the parking lot assisting the triage workers by checking pulses. Duke said during a recent interview, "I had been trained in CPR while in the US Navy. I was 23 at the time and had been out of the Navy less than a year, about 11 months, and my brother was only 20. That was such a difficult day, many untrue rumors about cover-ups filled the streets, and I ended up facing a great deal of ridicule from members of the community."

> **People who were not there have a hard time understanding. Duke said, "We did everything possible to save those prisoners."**

"The jail fire was just an unimaginable situation that left me and many others dealing with PTSD. I recall that it really hit me hard about one year later, and my sounding board to help talk me through it was Daily Herald Reporter Fred Chappell. I'm very grateful for his willingness to listen.

"Within the next few years, I moved away from Maury County and eventually from Tennessee. One of the primary reasons was the way members of the community looked at me and classified me in a negative way, as if I were responsible for the deaths that day. They looked at us all that way.

"My wife's father, was a very good man, but he even refused to walk his daughter down the aisle at our wedding because of me being at the jail fire. It was a number of years before he finally accepted me as a member of the family"

Deputy James George Hanvy worked the night shift at the time. He and Deputy Wendell Harris had picked up Zinmer during their last shift. Hanvy was at home in bed when the fire broke out. One of his friends called to check on him and told him about the fire. He immediately went in to offer assistance. Hanvy shared the following memories of that day, "I arrived and began doing everything I could to try and save lives. I worked with the firefighters who were getting people out of the facility. There were police officers, firefighters, sheriff's dept. employees and people from the funeral homes there to help.

"I first went in with just a face mask. But that didn't work out so well and I had to get an air pack. We were all on our hands and knees feeling our way around from one cell to another. Each of us taking the first person we came to and dragging them to the door on the west side of the jail where the triage unit was set up. We began in the workhouse area as that was the closest to the entrance doors and where the largest number of inmates would have been.

"The smoke was still so thick and visibility so poor, the people who I was working with, had me take the lead whenever we would move into a different area because I knew the facility. As we crawled using the walls as a guide they would at times hold onto my leg so as not to lose their way.

"Afterward we worked our way toward the cells on the east end of the corridor near the padded cell. Once all of the injured had been transported to the hospital, I was one of many who went to the hospital to help identify the victims."

Deputy Duke is shown here inside the padded cell wearing his street clothes. He had been off-duty and was only there at the jail by a twist of fate.

Duke's brother Larry Duke was serving in the US Air Force at the time of the fire. He was so impacted by this event, that after getting out of the Air Force, he went to work for the Columbia Fire Dept. where he served our community for over 30-years.

Hanvy mentioned that, "None of us had any idea that the smoke we were wandering through was toxic. Today if a similar type of fire were to occur, every rescue worker would be required to wear a hazardous material suit. Back then we just didn't know about the toxins.

"One positive thing that resulted from that horrible day was that it forced all entities responsible for penal institutions, to review the materials that were inside their facilities. It changed the way jails are constructed and administered."

A report compiled in March of 2010 by the NFPA Fire Analysis and Research Division, titled Prisons and Jails, states that since 1980 structure fires in prisons and jails have fallen 86%. Much of that reduction may very well be attributed to the fire safety code changes that resulted from the Maury County fire.

Memories of a Police Officer

Harvey Fischer was a police officer with the Columbia Police Department. At the time, Fischer worked the night shift in the downtown area. He recalls the following events that are related to the jail fire.

"I was working the night shift on Friday, June 24, 1977, when a pedestrian waved me over. He mentioned that he had just been out on the interstate and pulled over for a hitchhiker, to give him a ride, however, he drove away and did not pick the young man up because it seemed like something was very wrong with him.

"I then called my dispatch who turned the matter over to the Maury County Sheriff's Department since the interstate area is well outside the jurisdiction of the City Police Department.

"I later learned that the hitchhiker was Andy Zinmer.

> **"Early Sunday afternoon I got a call from the City Dispatch Officer, who I thought said there was a <u>jailbreak</u> occurring at the Maury County Jail."**

"I immediately headed in, which was a quick trip as I lived in the downtown area. I stopped by the city jail to pick up my baton and riot gear, and then headed down the street to the county jail.

"When I arrived Frank Duncan was already there, he too was under the impression that a prison break was occurring and had shown up with an automatic weapon. We didn't figure out until we were already there that the issue was a jail fire and not a **jailbreak**."

Pictured below is Frank Duncan outside the jail.

"I remember seeing Doug Young, a Vietnam Veteran who I knew worked for Oakes & Nichols, there giving mouth-to-mouth to victims. Bunny Sowell, also from Oakes & Nichols was there as well, as was Junior Gray with his wrecker knocking holes in walls.

"Later in the day Sargent Pat Troope called and asked me to go to the hospital and help get fingerprints and photographs of the victims. Out there with us was TBI Agent Andrew Earl and others.

"I will never forget the smell of smoke and death inside that temporary morgue. Over the next few days, I assisted with much of the work that went on at Oakes & Nichols as I am related to the Sowell family by marriage.

"It was a sad time for our community. A time that will not be forgotten by anyone who was involved."

Memories of Firefighters

Firefighters from Columbia Fire Department station one were on the scene just ninety-seconds after the call came in. One of those firefighters was **Don Martin**.

Martin spoke with me at length regarding his experiences that day. "We were the first team to arrive and as we pulled up I saw thick, black plumes of smoke coming from the east end of the facility, and sitting in the east parking lot, under deputy guard, was a young male burn victim.

"Burns were observable on his upper torso, shoulder, and back, as he sat shivering in the 90-degree heat, as if he were cold. I later learned that was Andy Zinmer.

"Two of us were immediately sent inside to locate the missing keys. As we entered the facility we encountered thick, black smoke, with large pieces of soot floating through the air. The smoke was so dark and dense that the light from my heavy-duty flashlight looked more like a cigarette tip than a flashlight.

> **"I had never before, or since, seen smoke that thick, dark, and soot-filled. It was unreal, you could not see, and we had to feel our way around through the pitch black, darkness. It was like crawling through an unfamiliar building with my eyes closed."**

The two firefighters crawled on their hands and knees, feeling their way through the darkness, searching for the keys, as the other firefighters brought in the fire-extinguishing agents and began working on putting out the fire which was limited to the padded cell. A water hose, dropped in through the roof vent to the cell effectively doused the flames.

"My partner and I were still frantically searching for the keys as many prisoners were rattling their cell doors and calling for help. As mere minutes passed, those sounds became more and more silent. That toxic smoke was claiming it's victims.

"Firefighter Jim Swindle located the keys and was working in the darkness to match keys to each cell door. At that point, our task changed to getting people out. I started by grabbing the first person I came to and dragging them to the triage area, before crawling back through the darkness to locate another victim.

> **"Each person was completely covered in soot. It was evident to me that the fire had been petroleum based. That's the only thing that would produce that combination of smoke and soot."**

"I was in my early twenties at the time, and in good physical condition, however, that was a challenge even for me, as we pulled one after another, out into fresh air. I couldn't tell one person from another as everyone, and everything inside that jail was concealed in black soot. I was just grabbing whoever I came to first and pulling as hard as I could, to get them out to medical help.

"Just prior to my second tank of oxygen running out, I ended up in an ambulance myself, and I spent the next two days at the Maury County hospital recovering from the inhalation of noxious fumes. The design of the demand-air packs that were used in 1977, was imperfect, and some of those toxins were allowed in.

"It was a very long time before I could sleep well. Especially since station one of the Fire Department was located just above the city jail, and whenever any prisoner would start yelling and rattling a jail door during the night, I would awake with a start and immediately experience flashbacks of that horrific day.

"Firefighters spend a great amount of time training on how to **save lives**. I came away from the jail fire with a huge amount of stress, anxiety, and feelings of intense remorse.

"Feelings of inadequacy and disappointment in myself for not having been able to do more.

"Looking back, I realize now that I, and many others, were dealing with post-traumatic stress disorder (PTSD), but in 1977, people didn't talk about that."

> **"Men especially were all expected to just get up and move on. So, get up and move on was what we all did but, I can assure you that not one person involved in that event has forgotten, or even fully recovered, from being there."**

"I seriously considered leaving the fire department for some time after that fire. As much as I loved my job, that event was life-altering for us all. I just didn't know if I could go through something like that again"

Wink Brown, a firefighter from Williamson County made the following comment, "I was on the scene about 15 minutes after the call went out. I was involved in the removal. By the time I got there, there was mass confusion on the radios, but on the scene, it was pretty well organized."

The Fire Chief of the Columbia Fire Department at the time was Bob Maddox, however, **Ruben Butler**, then Assistant Chief, was in charge during the event. Butler submitted a four-page, hand-written report of the jail fire. Portions of that report are provided below:

"The alarm was received by the Columbia Fire Dept. at 1:55 PM on Sunday, June 26, 1977. Our response was immediate with pumpers # 1, and # 6, with a total of 8 men and Assistant Chief. These men consisted of 1 Captain, 2 drivers, and 5 firefighters.

"I arrived only a few seconds before the pumpers and as I surveyed the scene, there was dense, black, heavy smoke coming out of the doors around the dispatcher office. The smoke was more-dense on the east side and smoke was coming from all vents and small openings in the east wing. No flame was visible.

"I immediately told Capt. McCall to put two charged lines in the front in the small windows in the east wing and have the other 3 men put on air masks. One man had just made exit into the east parking area covered with soot and showing signs of possible burns.

"He sat down next to the front of the building and appeared to be in fair condition. About this time, we were told by deputy Dickey that the keys had been lost in the panic and it became apparent that rescue would be a problem, if not impossible.

"In the meantime, I had called for all available men and for any air tanks and masks that could be found.

"By this time Grays wrecker service had arrived on the scene, and with two masonry saws and a sledgehammer I had gotten from station 1, they, with help available began breaking through the wall of the east wing.

"As soon as the hole on the east wing was large enough for entrance, those men and tools moved to work on the wall of the north wing."

The first hole granted access to the maximum security cell, and the hole in the north end would've provided access to the main jail and workhouse area.

The report went on to state that firefighter Swindle located the keys on the floor of the dispatch office. This was perplexing for me until I clarified with the dispatcher, who had been on duty, that the east door heading into the corridor and the east door to the dispatch office were both standing wide open.

One or more of the 30 visitors rushing to exit had kicked the brass keys and the dispatch office was where they landed.

The following diagram indicates the paths of escape that were available to 38 of the visitors who were inside the jail. Dickey had dropped to the floor in the 7' wide corridor area indicated on the diagram with the keys in his hand, and was crushed against the wall as 30 panicked visitors rushed to escape.

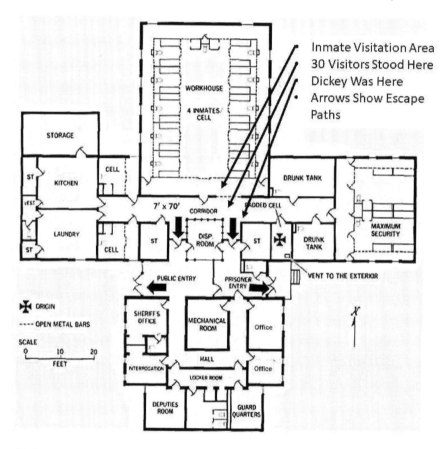

Inmate Visitation Area
30 Visitors Stood Here
Dickey Was Here
Arrows Show Escape Paths

"All on-duty firefighters, as well as all of those off-duty who were called in, worked to the point of exhaustion. Six were carried to the hospital, Martin, Swindle, Isabell, Frierson, Potts, and Benefield. Potts, Isabell, and Martin were kept overnight.

"The valuable help of many concerned citizens is greatly appreciated, and I am sure, helped reduce the number of lives lost." The report was signed by Reuben Butler, Asst. Chief C Shift, Columbia Fire Dept. One correction to the report is that firefighter Martin ended up staying in the hospital for two days.

Firefighter Robert McCord and Captain Tommy Dooley reported in the shaded area A, shown in the diagram below, which was unlocked and standing open, were two bodies, one male, and one female. The firefighters were not aware of their identity, however, they were found in the hallway outside the cell of Buck Rowland.

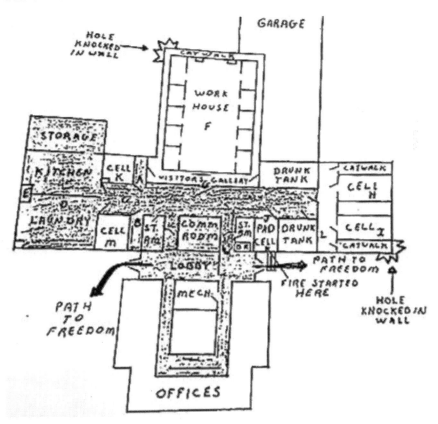

One male was located in the shaded area B, which was also unlocked and open to the corridor. This area was outside the women's cell where Janice Golden was incarcerated. Two males were found in a bathroom located in shaded area E. This area was also unlocked. This accounts for five of the eights visitors who were not locked in. The previous diagram was created by reporter Mark Wynn.

Off-duty **Firefighter Steve Secrest** stated that he and other firefighters carried two out of in front of the last cell inside the workhouse, near the last table located in area F. He also said that several victims were found inside or just outside of their cells. Access to these people had been gained through the hole that was knocked into the exterior wall.

Shown here is Firefighter Ben Frierson, who was off-duty at the time, but had responded to the urgent call for all firefighters to report in, being assisted out of the facility. Frierson was then taken to the hospital where he was treated for smoke inhalation.

Firefighter Ben Frierson was one of the first to enter the hole in the east side of the building. He reported at the time that he used a sledgehammer to break the lock from the catwalk into section L. This is where he found an older male, identified later as Luther Bellanfant, who was the only visitor behind a locked door.

Frierson attempted to break the lock on the cell where Lanny Bellanfant was housed, however, the sledgehammer messed up the lock. A torch was later used to access that cell. A key was used to access cell H, and victims were removed from that cell as a torch was being used on the door of cell I.

That horrific jail fire resulted in officials not only looking to the future but also reassessing some of the events in the past.

Fire Inspector Wayne Hickman told a Daily Herald reporter at the time that the fire department responded to a fire in the northern section of the city, off of Highway 31N, approximately three years prior to the jail fire. Hickman reported "There was a middle-aged couple who perished, and it was ruled that they died of carbon monoxide poisoning. Now, since the jail fire, we've thought a lot about that earlier fire and the possibility that the two victims may have died from poisonous gasses, the same as some of the prisoners.

"There was black sooty residue found at the house where the two people died, and the jail fire makes us think that these type of fumes may have claimed lives in homes where there are many plastic products. It's the synthetics that are killing people, although, I'm not saying all plastic products are producing the same type of gases."

Memories of am EMS Worker

I recently spoke with **Freddie Rich**, former Director of the Maury County Emergency Communications District regarding his memories of that day.

"At the time, the EMS station was located directly behind the Maury County Hospital.

I was at the station when the dispatch call came is from Ms. Johnnie Webb, at the Columbia Police Department.

> **"I wasn't certain if she had said jail fire or jail fight, so I quickly called to clarify. She confirmed it was a fire."**

"Two of our units were immediately dispatched to the scene. I was the first EMS worker to arrive at the jail. The first of the injured that I attended to was Andy Zinmer, the young kid who started that deadly fire. When I arrived, I found him lying in the jail parking lot with a deputy standing over him.

"Inside the jail, the smoke was so thick and dark, hovering six to eight inches above the floor, leaving very little breathable air. Having worked for a number of years as a firefighter. I've experienced numerous fire situations, however, I've never seen smoke like that. It was dark black, thick, and even had flickers of yellow and green floating in it.

"A triage unit was set up in the parking lot where I provided medical care until the doctors, and other medical attendants, arrived from the local hospital.

"On my first trip to the hospital, I utilized the ambulance radio and asked if someone with a scanner, that was picking up my signal, would call the Maury County Hospital and inform them that we would be bringing in as many as 100 patients. I did this so that they could call some doctors in. At that time, the hospital did not maintain doctors on staff during the weekends and the odds of any being there on a Sunday afternoon were pretty slim.

"I knew a lot of people were at the Oak Park pool that day so I had an announcement issued there for all off-duty EMS personnel to report in. Two of them showed up still wearing their swimsuits.

"Ambulances were called in from all the surrounding counties, and we transported seventy-five people that day, to the local hospital, as we raced against the clock to save as many lives as possible. At one point one of the EMS workers in the back of my unit was doing CPR on two victims at once by working on one for a time and then switching to the other. Almost everyone who worked on the scene that day required some level of oxygen treatment.

Pictured below left to right are EMTs Ray Oliver, Freddie Rich, and Bill Hord.

"Local funeral homes also assisted in transporting victims to the hospital, using their typically pristine hearses as black, soot-ridden, ambulances.

"Zinmer was one that needed to be transported to Vanderbilt Hospital in Nashville. There was no such thing as life flight then, so the Fort Campbell Army base in Clarksville, TN was contacted. They sent four helicopters to transport Zinmer and other victims, to Nashville hospitals."

> **"There were many amazing acts of service that occurred that day. At one point Boy Scouts were assisting the TN National Guard with traffic control. Members of the Maury County Civil Defense were there. Everyone was doing what they could to help."**

"During my last trip from the hospital back to the jail, a vehicle turned, from a lane of stopped traffic, onto the shoulder of the road just as I was rushing past with sirens on. My EMS unit landed on the hood of that car.

"My partner and I immediately jumped out to give care for those who were injured. That was our job, that's just what we did. I didn't really think much about the  damage to the EMS unit itself. My concern was for the people in that car, who were not replaceable. We had lost enough that day and did not need to add to the number of lost souls."

Memories of Nurses

Patsy Cross Smotherman was on her way to work at Maury County Hospital. It was a beautiful, sunny afternoon as she drove with the car windows down and music blaring, from her orange Chevy Vega. As she topped the Trotwood Ave. bridge over the railroad tracks, she saw an ambulance with its lights on, and siren shrieking, racing toward her. She knew then that it was not going to be a typical lazy Sunday at the hospital.

She was excited about the day as it was her first opportunity to work as a Nurse Tech, in the new emergency room which was roughly ten times larger, and much more advanced than the small facility she was accustomed to working in.

Soon after entering the ER to begin her shift the "red" phone started ringing. That phone was a dedicated line reserved for ambulance-service only use, and its loud, urgent ring was continuous until answered. Smotherman said "I quickly grabbed the phone and heard EMT Freddie Rich say, I'm bringing in a 16-year old with burns and smoke inhalation. There will probably be 40 or 50 more coming, and all of a sudden ambulances started arriving from everywhere."

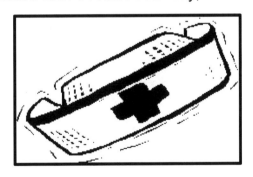

"I was not involved in providing care for Zinmer who was the only actual burn victim brought in. Each of the other patients brought in were dealing with the inhalation of toxic smoke. It just so happened that a pulmonary lung expert was on staff that day. That was a blessing.

"The National Guard quickly roped off the area outside the ER but I clearly recall a little, old, lady, who probably weighed only 90 pounds come in searching for her grandson. I have no idea how she got past the National Guard.

"The entire event seemed like a dream as I ran from one to another putting on oxygen masks. We didn't follow the typical process of gathering names, insurance information or even checking blood pressure. It was a matter of providing care as quickly as possible to all.

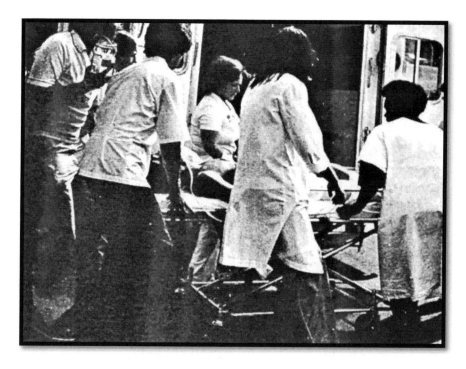

"Each person was covered with soot and I remember it almost looked as though their bodies and hair were dipped in dark coal dust.

Janet Meadows had been a nurse for four months when the jail fire occurred. She, her mother, and sister were all nurses and were all working that fateful day. She and her mother were walking into the ER together that afternoon when they heard an ambulance, then four ambulances, and then it seemed like ambulances were everywhere.

"Lots of patients came in at one time and appeared to be covered in thick, black soot. We quickly began assisting in providing emergency care. Several patients required incubation (breathing tubes) and IVs.

"As anyone who has had an IV knows the injection site is cleaned first with an alcohol swab. That didn't work against that thick soot, I had to use a large towel and scrub to get the soot off so that an IV could be safely inserted.

"There were so many people. It was an extremely emotional day for all of us. A day that I will never forget. Our first priority was caring for the patients, this was followed by caring for the families, which was followed by dealing with the media.

"We were extremely fortunate to have a pulmonologist there that day. It was his last scheduled day to work at the Maury County Hospital. All of the victims who survived required his care in the Intensive Care Unit.

"We were also fortunate that this event didn't occur when we were in the 4-bed Emergency Department. I don't know how we could've handled that situation in that old facility. I recall that we had twelve people in cardiac arrest at the same time, and we were resuscitating many patients who showed signs of having soot in their windpipes."

Smotherman commented that, "After some time I finally returned to the desk, and a deputy in a white t-shirt walked up to the counter and asked for help with identifying the bodies of the ones who were lost. I offered to assist and went first to get some washcloths so that the soot could be wiped off each face. He also asked for some white tape that he could use to write names on.

"A make-shirt morgue had been set up inside the unfinished physical therapy room in a wing of the hospital that was still under construction. I was impressed with the deputy because as I washed faces, he immediately recognized each one, even the visitors. I knew one of the victims, Janice Golden. She and I went to school together and I knew she had blonde hair, but that day, it was jet black from the soot.

"Some of the bodies were damp and the deputy explained that many of the inmates crawled into the shower and let the water run until it ran out. He said that the water pipe supplying the main area of the jail had melted as a result of the fire and heat from the padded cell.

"I noticed as I wiped off each of the faces, there was no visible bleeding, bruising or injuries of any kind. Just black soot."

Meadows said, "By the time the majority of the victims had been identified, all of the family members had been moved to the hospital cafeteria, where they waited to learn the condition of their loved ones. A priest and a chaplain were there offering their services that evening to share difficult news with the family members.

> **"We all felt incredibly helpless, and tried to provide as much comfort as we could, even though, we knew it did little to relive their pain."**

"I recall that at some point during the evening the phone that was reserved for ambulance-service only use started ringing. I grabbed it and on the line was NBC New York News asking to speak with the Hospital Administrator. I have no idea how they were able to get that private number.

"It was around 10 PM when some of us had gathered in the utility room where burgers had been dropped off for us by the staff from Oakes and Nichols Funeral Home. We were all very weary and emotionally drained."

Smotherman said "It was a very long shift and I remember walking out of the ER where I was approached by news reporters from the Nashville Banner. My comments, and photograph landed on the front page of that paper the following morning.

> **"Even though Zinmer was the only burn victim that day, and I was not directly involved in his care, I still to this day have flash-back memories when I treat burn victims, or when I smell burning wood. It's because of the intense smoke smell. I will never forget that terrible day."**

Shown next are numerous hearses lined up in a field outside the Maury County Hospital.

Smotherman went on to say, "Sometime later, after Zinmer had recovered and was back in the Maury County Jail, I was working the night shift when some of the jail inmates roughed Zinmer up. The injuries he sustained were not significant, but he was brought into the ER for treatment, and I was the nurse who attended him. My memory of the boy is that he was very quiet, and would not make eye contact with anyone.

"As Zinmer was being released from the hospital, there were numerous reporters outside, near the awaiting patrol car. I grabbed a sheet and placed it over his head to cover him up. He spoke to me for the first time then and said thank you." That was my only encounter with Andy Zinmer.

Memories of News Reporters

Mark Wynn, a well-known reporter and photographer for the Columbia Daily Herald at the time was on sight as the tragedy unfolded, and he has numerous vivid memories of the event.

"I was standing at the front door of the jail as the victims were brought out. As I was photographing the scene, I watched as paramedics provided CPR to so very many. You couldn't tell what race anyone was because of all the dark, black, soot. I had interviewed many of the inmates in the jail at one point, but I was having a hard time identifying anyone there, with one exception. When Buck Rowland was brought out and laid directly at my feet, I did recognize him. Buck was a nice guy, but, he had a troubled history.

"That event was the worst jail fire in the history of the state, and it remains the most devastating jail fire in Tennessee history to this day.

"Interviewing survivors later on at the local hospital resulted in many stories of heroism. One story was about an older man, a known bank robber, who was trapped in the main cell block area where the majority of the prisoners were. He was helping the other inmates wrap wet towels around their heads. By doing that, he saved many lives that day, but sadly, lost his own."

Another vivid memory Wynn carries from that day was being with his former high school classmate Chavez McClarn at the local hospital. Wynn recalled standing on the front lawn of the Maury County Hospital beside a gurney where McClarn laid as he waited for the helicopter from Fort Campbell to take him to a hospital in Nashville for treatment of severe inhalation of toxic smoke.

> "It was a weird moment as I was no longer a reporter, but just a friend, there supporting another friend. I recall holding his hand and telling him that everything would be ok. I have no clue if he even remembers me being there because he was in really bad shape. In out of consciousness at the time."

A few of the many photographs taken at the scene that day are shown here, courtesy of Mark Wynn and the Columbia Daily Herald. Below is an unnamed, fatigued, firefighter.

Here an unnamed paramedic is doing CPR on a victim.

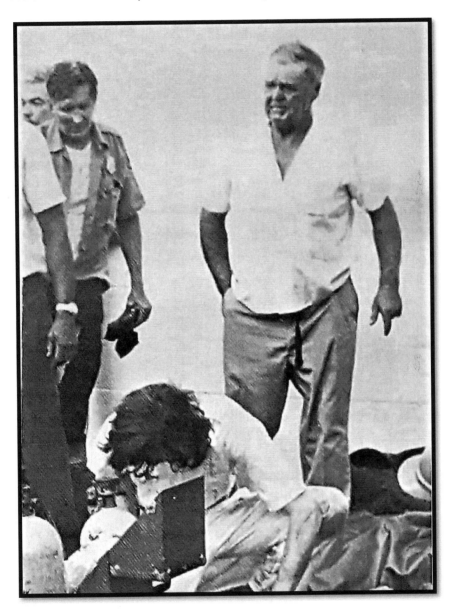

Next is a horrific parking lot scene.

Fred Chappell, who passed away in 2012, was at one time a reporter for the Columbia Daily Herald. The Herald published an article written by Chappell 16 years after the fire. Portions of that article are included herein.

"The events of that Sunday are burned in my brain forever; it is like the smell of smoke that clings to your clothes long after the fire is out.

"When I heard the first call for fire trucks and ambulances needed at Maury County Jail, I did not believe the relatively new jail, constructed of concrete and steel, could be on fire. It wasn't actually on fire, I found when I arrived 15 minutes after the first alarm sounded."

Inside firefighters could see nothing because of the smoke and the fact that the fire and intense heat had shorted the electrical system.

"Suited with air packs and flashlights, firemen searched for victims and the keys to the cells. Their lights blinked in the darkness like lightning bugs in a black storm.

"There was a desperate shout of "Bugger" as firemen groped in the smoke looking for one of their own because his air pack alarm was ringing somewhere inside the 7' x 70' corridor. The darkness was impenetrable.

"Even after the keys were located, it was difficult to match keys with locks, but those rescue workers did not give up until every single person was brought out. One by one, each victim was pulled through the darkness, to the west exit, where the triage unit could take over.

> **"CPR was administered to the unconscious and shouts of "breathe, dammit, breathe" could be heard above the slaps of CPR being performed. Life was restored to the lucky ones."**

"The pile of empty yellow air tanks was soon joined by a rising number of zipped black plastic body bags."

Harvey Mason was a radio news director with WMCP at the time of the fire and was one of the first reporters on the scene.

However, instead of reporting he quickly found himself in the role of a participant, giving mouth-to-mouth resuscitation to one apparently lifeless man who had been carried out on a stretcher from the smoke-filled building.

Mason said at the time, "I have no idea who he was. One of the doctors said somebody do something, so I worked on him for three or four minutes. I was breathing into him and after the third time he started breathing and bit my finger which was holding down his tongue."

Having learned CPR in 1967 while serving in the US Navy, this was the first time he had ever performed the life-saving technique. "And believe me," Mason commented, "the real thing was different."

Memories of a Funeral Director

I recently had the opportunity to speak with **Tony Sowell** from the Oakes & Nichols Funeral Home. Sowell said, "We had a funeral service going on that Sunday afternoon and had a real challenge trying to get the funeral procession out onto West 7th Street because of all the traffic and emergency vehicles traveling back and forth from the jail to the hospital.

"We took a detour as the funeral procession made its way to the cemetery, in order to avoid the hospital area, so as not to interfere with any of the numerous emergency vehicles. After the interment at the cemetery, Sowell changed roles and put his hearse into action as an ambulance, transporting victims from the jail to the hospital.

> **"I've been in the funeral business all my life. Death is not new to me, but, when I walked into that makeshift morgue at the hospital that Sunday afternoon, the site of 42 bodies laid out in one room, took my breath away. That is something that I will never forget."**

"We provided funeral services for many of the victims and had to keep the news reporters at bay because, in my opinion, reporters have no business inside the funeral home, and they were not permitted inside our facility. This was a place where family members were grieving.

"Surprisingly, there were no deaths as a result of burns. Out of all the victims we cared for during that event, only one had an injury, and that was Buck Rowland. Buck had fallen inside his cell shower and incurred a hematoma, (commonly known as a goose egg) on his forehead."

Below is a scene outside the church where the Rowland and Anderson family service was held, and next are hearses on the way to the cemetery.

"I recall one funeral service that we facilitated where some of the family members stepped outside to be interviewed. That was their choice, but it would not have been appropriate for reporters to be allowed inside. I don't care how big of a news story it was."

In spite of their best efforts, one reporter evidently did make his way inside to snap the photo below of a grieving family member.

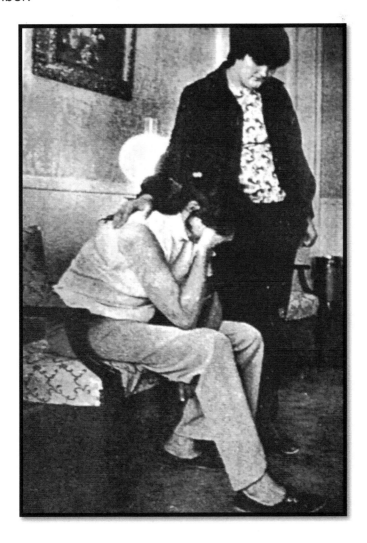

Community Impact

The healing process for the community continues to this day. The event altered so many lives in a matter of a few moments.

Columbia had previously experienced two notable fires. In 1949 a fire erupted backstage in the Princess Theater. The theater and the luxurious Bethel House Hotel were built in 1882 and the two shared a common wall. That fire resulted in the loss of the theater, hotel, and the entire city block. Shown below are the hotel on the right and the theater to the left.

In addition, the Columbia Institute, a former school for girls burned to the ground in 1954. Shown next is that facility as it once stood proudly on West 7th Street, where now the US Post Office, and Harris Foodland can be found.

Neither of those events, as bad as they were, could begin to compare to the devastation of the Maury County Jail Fire. The emotional damage was deep and intense.

As many members of our community began attending multiple funeral services, Judge Taylor Rayburn was quoted as saying "This is the worst catastrophe this town has ever had."

Our community lost many good people that day. Most of the victims were not hardened criminals, but, had been imprisoned for relatively minor offenses.

One was being held for not wearing his glasses while driving and could've been freed by paying a $39.50 fine. Four were charged with other driving charges such as DUI and driving without a license. Two were charged with public drunkenness and could have been released on payment of a $24.50 fine.

There were four others who were charged with the same offense, however, their fines were higher, ranging up to $39.50.

At the hospital that afternoon was Rev. Robert Tharp. He was one of ministers who were there consoling the families. Tharp was quoted as saying, "The grief was very apparent. We found a great deal of shock and disbelief it had happened."

The Tuesday following that fateful Sunday was when the first of the visitations and funerals began. Out of respect for those who were lost, County Judge Taylor Rayburn had the bells in the courthouse tower tolling every five minutes. That solemn tolling of the bells echoed throughout the town for many days, as the entire community was enveloped in profound mourning.

Pictured above is the Maury County Courthouse. That regal and majestic building still sits in the middle of the square in downtown Columbia, just a couple of blocks from the old jail. I remember those mournful bell tolls for the souls that were lost in 1977 whenever I am downtown at the top of the hour, and those same bells ring out. The sound still reverberates across the sky today, just as it did in 1977.

A community service of intercession and affirmation was held on Wednesday, June 29th at the Columbia First Presbyterian Church. With the church located just a couple of blocks from the jail, then Pastor John Kaufman was quoted as saying "The Christian faith was born in tragedy and from that tragedy arose the faith that the sovereignty of God transcends tragedy and even death itself.

"This past weekend our community suffered a severe tragedy and it's appropriate that our Christian faith speaks to that tragedy. Therefore, several churches in our area have arranged this community worship service." Pictured is the First Presbyterian Church, where that prayer service was held.

The intention of that special community service was to offer prayers for those who suffered loss and also prayers for the loss suffered by our community. The service was also meant to affirm our faith in God who will sustain us through all.

Numerous groups, such as the Social Security Administration, Department of Veterans Affairs, the South Central Human Resources Agency, and the American Red Cross, all worked to ensure that the family members of victims were aware of both the services and the financial assistance, that could be made available to them.

Hooper Penuel from the Tennessee Department of Veterans affairs said at the time that, "Some of the families might be eligible for Veterans benefits." Officials from that office visited many funeral homes, jails, and hospitals to assist in securing information regarding benefit qualification. "Prisoners or visitors who received honorable discharges are eligible for burial benefits. We will also be able to secure flags for burials if there are not enough. We will be trying to help in any way we can."

Additionally, County Judge Taylor Rayburn sent a request to the Tennessee Civil Defense Department to determine if there were any other State or Federal assistance programs that might be made available for the victims and their families.

The Aftermath

The Maury County Quarterly Court's Jail Committee agreed to establish an unbiased committee of Maury County residents, with no governmental affiliation, to facilitate an independent investigation of the jail fire.

For the committee to be viewed as fair and unprejudiced, they needed to be selected by the community itself, instead of the members being appointed by the Jail Committee, therefore, Judge Rayburn's office reached out to two local ministerial organizations, the Maury County Medical Association, the Board of Education, Columbia State Community College, a labor organization, a local farm organization, the Chamber of Commerce, two industries for chemical engineers, and one professional women's club.

Each organization was asked to recommend one person who would participate as a member of this committee. The group was to be given unrestricted access and great latitude to fully investigate the incident. They could ask any questions, of any person. The only real caveat was that their final report was to be submitted to the court and made available to the public at the same time.

As the committee was established, numerous lawsuits were being filed against the County, and the attorneys representing Sheriff Voss and County employees advised those involved not to discuss the incident at that time. The lawsuits prompted an investigation by the Grand Jury.

Independent Committee member, Reverend Bob Tharp, had agreed to facilitate the role of temporary Chairman, for the committee to allow time for the permanent chairman to be selected, however, a decision to recess the committee was reached on Wed. July 27, 1977. The group felt it would be more appropriate to wait until the Grand Jury investigation was completed.

Committee member James Burt, said at the time, "If we are not able to speak to some of the people involved, we are limited in what we can do."

Unfortunately, those lawsuits continued over the course of the next 8 years. By that time, there was nothing of value that the committee could offer.

The jail was initially left uninhabitable for a number of months after the fire. During that time, the County shared facilities with the City while decisions were made about going forward.

Below, from left to right, three of the twelve members of the Maury County Quarterly Court who toured the jail shortly after the incident are pictured, Charles Tisher, Bobby Harris, and William English.

I recently spoke with Charles Tisher and asked about his memories of the jail fire. His singular comment, as he looked down and shook his head was, "It was just a horrible, horrible thing that happened."

> **Mr. William English said at the time, "I doubt I could've found my way out of there, even as familiar as I am with the jail. I'm surprised there weren't more deputies hurt.**

"I wish everyone could go through the jail and see the whole situation. We've got to convince a lot of people what happened. A tour would explain exactly what caused the situation."

English was one of the many people who watched the events unfold that Sunday afternoon from across the street, and he was back at the jail, first thing on the following Monday to tour the facility.

Bobby Harris, who was then Chairman of the Jail Workhouse Committee said, "It is a horrible situation and it was bound to have been hell for anyone in there."

Those touring the jail witnessed the destruction inside and saw the once clear glassed-in-windows of the dispatch office that looked as if they had been painted black. There was a layer of ash 1/2" to 1" thick on the benches. Mattresses were still laying partially over toilet bowls where some of the inmates had been trying to avoid inhaling the smoke.

Then Governor Ray Blanton established a five-person task force to review the Maury County jail fire, He is quoted as stating; "When you have 42-persons dead in a few minutes, you need to know why."

Sheriff Voss mentioned that even one of the trustees who was very accustomed to coming and going within and outside of the jail, was not able to find his way out when he had been located only a few feet from the exit.

> **English also added the following
> "I've heard all kinds of flak and wild
> rumors from people, but if you've been
> through it like I've been through it, they
> would see it in a different light."**

I knew Mr. English personally for many years. He and my late father worked together at the Monsanto Chemical Co. and I had the pleasure of knowing Mr. English as a member of a credit union where I worked in the early 90's. Mr. English left this earth in January of 2017 and I can tell you that he was one of the most honorable men I have ever met. One thing that I can say with absolute confidence is this. **Anything that Mr. English said could be taken as absolute truth. There was not one dishonest bone in his body.**

As mentioned previously, the majority of the prisoners being held at the time were there for minor infractions. Sheriff Bill Voss began working with local Judges to place many inmates on probation or suspend the sentences of City and County inmates. This was primarily due to the extremely limited capacity of the City jail with its 3 to 4 cells. Thus freeing up space in the for the inmates who had more serious charges.

Some inmates were transferred to surrounding county jail facilities, while others remained in the few cells located in the Columbia City Jail.

Since that dreadful day, there have been numerous changes made to national fire-safety codes. Many of those changes were a direct result of the tragedy that occurred here. In truth, the fire itself was small, however, the toxic smoke was what caused the loss of life.

Safety code changes have considerably reduced the odds of this sort of tragedy ever being repeated. One very significant change included ridding jails of mattresses, and padded cells, that contain polyurethane which ignites easily dispersing toxic, deadly fumes.

Bill Wamsley, Director of the Fire Marshal's engineering plans review section, stated that the pre-Columbia fire safety code included only 1 1/2 pages on how life safety should be applied to jails. Today there are 15 in-depth pages.

A report compiled by the National Fire Protection Association on the 1977 jail fire identified three major factors contributing to the multiple loss of life:

1. The presence of a fuel that, once ignited, produced an extreme amount of smoke rapidly.

2. The failure to extinguish the fire in its incipient stage.
3. The absence of any means for quickly and reliably protecting inmates and visitors, either by evacuation to a secure place of refuge in the building, or through incremental measures of defense against fire while remaining in the main cell block.

Lawsuits brought by the families of victims, drug on for about 8 years. The final payout by insurance companies made on behalf of Maury County, and companies that manufactured the polyurethane, was reportedly about $1.5 million.

There are understandably still many unresolved, and troubled feelings over this tragedy. It is not for me to comprehend the workings of our universe, but I can learn to accept what we cannot change, and move forward in some meaningful way.

It is my wish to ensure that this event is never forgotten and it's because of that I contacted Tom Price, the Director of the Maury County Archives, and asked that he work with me to establish a memorial marker at the site.

My hope is that we will soon have that memorial marker in place to document the event, and honor the victims by listing the name, and date of birth, of each precious soul that was lost that day.

Families Lost

Of the 42 souls lost, each person was a beloved member of a family, however, the loss hit some families in greater numbers than it did others.

The Bellanfants

Ira Lane (Lanny) Bellanfant was arrested on serious charges and was being held in a maximum security cell. His father, Luther Bellanfant Jr. had arrived late for the visiting hour but was allowed in. The exception was made by Chief Deputy Farmer.

Bellanfant Jr. would've been visiting his son in the maximum security cell area to the east of the padded cell. He was the

only visitor locked inside the facility and, just like all other visitors there that day, was a mere five minutes from the end of the visitation hour.

Both Ira and Luther Bellanfant Jr. were laid to rest in Wilkes Cemetery in Culleoka, TN.

The Goldens

Both Calvin Golden Jr. and his wife Janice Boswell Webb Golden were inmates at the time of the fire. Calvin was 22 years old and Janice was 2-days away from celebrating her 23rd birthday, and release from jail. There visiting the two of them were Calvin's parents, Ralph Calvin Golden Sr. and Shirley DeWilde Golden, with their daughter, Dorothy (Dottie) Golden Wright.

Calvin Jr. and the visiting family members were standing outside the women's cell where Janice was incarcerated. Although Calvin Jr. was an inmate, in his role as trustee, he was allowed to move in and out of the facility. He knew the layout of the jail very well, however, the toxic smoke was so thick, Golden must've been completely disoriented as when the fire broke out, he and others were only a matter of feet from the exit to the lobby.

All five members of the Golden family perished that dreadful day. Janice was in her cell, one male was found in the small hallway outside her cell, while the others, in an attempt to escape, made a wrong turn and were later found inside the laundry room.

The Golden family members are buried together in a mass-grave in Rose Hill Cemetery. Next is a picture of the custom-designed, triple-heart stone maker for Dottie Golden Wright, and her parents Ralph and Shirley Golden, that is connected to a double-heart marker for Calvin and Janice Golden.

The beautiful headstone shown next was designed by a family member.

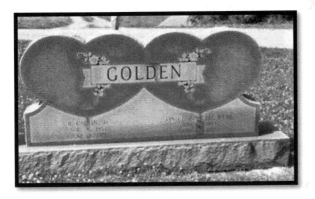

The Anderson and Rowland Families

Herman Anderson lost six members of his family that day. Five were at the jail visiting Anderson's son-in-law, William Henry "Buck" Rowland, Jr.

Lost that day were his wife, Mary Alice Anderson, daughter Margaret Alice Anderson Rowland, sons, Marvin W. Anderson and Billy H. Anderson, and sons-in-law, Rowland, and Frank Irwin.

The current Sheriff of Maury County, Bucky Rowland, lost six family members that day as well.

Rowland's father, William Henry "Buck" Rowland Jr., his mother Margaret Alice Anderson Rowland, his grandmother, Mary Alice Anderson, and uncles, Marvin W. Anderson, Billy H. Anderson, and Frank Irwin.

None of them escaped. Buck Rowland was found inside the shower of his cell, while one male and one female were found in the hallway just outside the cell. The location of where the other family members were found is unknown.

When asked about this during his 2014 campaign for Sheriff, Rowland was quoted as saying, "It's kind of like a Hallmark story," Rowland said. "You can't make this stuff up."

I asked Sheriff Rowland about the fire recently and if he was there in the lobby as some have believed. Rowland said, "No, I was told that my mother had intended to take me, however, being a typical 2 ½-year old I was being fussy that day, so my aunt, who ended up becoming my second mother, offered to keep me at home and fix a nice Sunday dinner for when the family returned." Sadly, that dinner was never enjoyed, as not one member of the Rowland family came back home that day.

After the jail fire, the 2 1/2 year-old Rowland was raised by his aunt, Carolyn Irwin. Mrs. Irwin was the widow of Frank Irwin who perished at the jail. She was also the sister of Sheriff Rowlands mother.

After that fateful day, she was left with her own four children, and three of her sister's children to raise. Shown next is the marker at the family grave for the Anderson and Rowland family members buried in Morrow Cemetery.

Next is the marker for Frank Irwin who is buried in Arlington Cemetery.

Shown below is the headstone for Buck Rowland who is buried at Polk Memorial Gardens.

May We Never Forget

May We Never Forget

June 26, 1977

Lost that day were our sons,

daughters, parents, grandparents,

brothers, sisters, aunts, uncles, and

dearly-loved friends.

These 42 precious souls listed below carried many different titles during their lives. I've tried to capture just a little bit about each person, and the various roles they would've held. Each one was a beloved member of a family.

Richard Amos was born on Nov. 4, 1952, and was a 24-year old son and brother from Maury County. Unemployed at the time of his death, Amos was survived by his father, four half-brothers, and two half-sisters. Services were held at Baxter Brothers Funeral Home. He had been charged with improper dress and possession of less than 1/2 oz. of marijuana.

Billy Herman Anderson, a visitor, was born on Aug. 23, 1940, and was a 36-year old son, and brother from the Williamsport area. He was survived by his father, two sisters, and two brothers. A family service was held at the Highland

Avenue Church of Christ. Along with other family members he was buried in Morrow Cemetery in Hampshire.

Mary Alice Bishop Anderson, a visitor, was born on Jul 28, 1914. She was a 62-year old wife, mother, grandmother, and sister from Williamsport. She was survived by her husband, two daughters, one sister, one brother, and 11 grandchildren. A family service was held at the Highland Avenue Church of Christ. Along with other family members she was buried in Morrow Cemetery in Hampshire.

Marvin Wayne Anderson, a visitor, was born on Feb. 22, 1946. He was a 31-year old husband, father, and brother from the Williamsport area. Anderson was survived by his wife, two daughters, and two sisters. A family service was held at the Highland Avenue Church of Christ. Along with other family members he was buried in Morrow Cemetery in Hampshire.

Benjamin Franklin Anthony was born on June 8, 1828, and was a brother who was survived by his two sisters and five brothers. Services were held at the First Baptist Church with the burial in Meadowlawn Memorial Gardens. Anthony was charged with trespassing, public drunkenness, and attempting to commit a felony.

John M. Baxter was born on Mar. 23, 1936. He was a farm-worker and son from Chapel Hill, TN and was survived only by his parents. Baxter lived and worked on the farm owned by his family. Services were held at Bills-McGaugh Funeral Home, with the burial in the Allen Cemetery in Caney Springs. The one charge filed against Baxter was vagrancy.

Ira Lane (Lanny) Bellanfant was born on Jan. 9, 1954 and was the 23-year old beloved son of Luther Bellanfant Jr. He lived on Hannaway Street in Columbia and was survived by his step-mother. Bellanfant was buried in Wilkes Cemetery in Culleoka, TN. The charges filed against him were 1st-degree burglary, auto theft, armed robbery, and two counts of kidnapping.

Luther Bellanfant Jr., a visitor, was born on June 6, 1914, and was a 63-year old husband, father, and grandfather from Culleoka. Mr. Bellanfant had been widowed in 1957. He was survived by his then wife Mattie, and his burial was in Wilkes Cemetery in Culleoka, TN.

Andrew Cannon was born on Nov. 16, 1931. He was a 45-year old son and brother from Water Street in Columbia who had served in the US Army during the Korean War. Cannon was survived by his father and a sister. Services were held at Mrs. A. J. Morton & Son Funeral Home with the burial in New Hope Cemetery. Cannon had been charged with public drunkenness.

Virginia Clara Cathey was born on Jan. 5, 1927. She was a 48-year old daughter, and sister from Polk Lane in Columbia. Cathey was survived by her father, two sisters, and a brother. Services were held at the Ryan Funeral Chapel with the burial in the Garden of Christianity at Pinecrest Memorial Gardens. Cathey had been charged with public drunkenness.

Roderick G. Cooper was born on July 13, 1948, and was a 28-year old laborer. Cooper was a son and brother from the Williamsport area. He was survived by his parents, a sister, two brothers, and one grandmother. His services were held at Claiborne Chapel A.M.E. Methodist Church, with the burial in Rosemount Cemetery. The charge filed against Cooper was public drunkenness.

Jerry Cross was born on May 5, 1951, and was a 26-year old laborer who lived on Riggins Row. Cross was a son, and brother who was survived by his mother, step-father, two sisters, and two brothers, and grandmothers. Services were held at Mrs. A. J. Morton & Sons Funeral Home with the burial in Centerville at Beech Wood Cemetery. The charges filed against Cross were malicious mischief and assault.

Terry Wayne Derryberry was born on July 28, 1956. He was a 20-year old son and brother from Dyer Street in Columbia. He was survived by his mother, step-father, two sisters, and a brother. Funeral services were held at Oakes & Nichols with the burial in the Garden of Everlasting Life at Polk Memorial Gardens. Derryberry was charged with 7-counts of passing worthless checks.

Lonnie Dean Fox was born on July 2, 1956. He was a 20-year old house-painter, husband, brother, and son from Brown Hollow Road in Columbia. Fox was survived by his wife, parents, two grandparents, and a brother. Services were held at McDonald Funeral Home in Centerville, with the burial in Totty's Bend Church of Christ Cemetery. Fox was charged with 3rd-degree burglary.

Thomas Eugene Frierson was born on Nov. 18, 1954, and was a 22-year old brother. Frierson was survived by one sister and eight brothers. His services were held at Baxter Brothers Funeral Home, with the burial in Rosemount Cemetery. He was one of three inmates who escaped 3-days prior to the jail fire and were apprehended in downtown Columbia, shortly after the escape. Frierson was charged with assault on an officer and armed robbery.

Ralph Calvin Golden Jr., was born on Nov. 8, 1954, and was a 22-year old husband, father, and brother from Culleoka. He was survived by a son, a sister, and a half-sister. Golden was working towards an early release and had lined up a job that he was scheduled to begin upon his release. The Golden family service was held at Oakes & Nichols Funeral Home, with a mass-grave, family burial in Rose Hill Cemetery. Golden had been charged with the possession and sale of a controlled substance.

Janice Faye Boswell Webb Golden was born on June 28, 1954. She was a 22-year old wife, mother, daughter, and sister from Culleoka. She was survived by one son, her parents, her step-father, one grandmother, and one brother. The Golden family service was held at Oakes & Nichols Funeral Home, with a mass-grave burial in Rose Hill Cemetery. Golden had been charged with DWI.

Ralph Calvin Golden Sr., a visitor, was born on Nov. 19, 1917. He was a 59-year old grandfather, father, son, and brother from Leoma. Mr. Golden was a welder and a mason who worked for the Chicago Bridge and Iron Company. He served as an SSGT in the US Army during WWII and was survived by two daughters, his father, two sisters, and three grandchildren.

Shirley Margaret Mary Dewilde Golden, a visitor, was born on March 23, 1930, in De Pere, Brown, WI. Mrs. Golden was 47-years old and was survived by two daughters, and three grandchildren. The Golden family service was held at Oakes & Nichols Funeral Home, with a mass-grave, family burial in Rose Hill Cemetery.

Andrew Haley was born on March 31, 1948 and was a 29-year old believed to be from Napier Court in Nashville. He is buried in the Nashville National Cemetery. Haley had been charged with grand larceny.

William Edward Howell was born on Jan. 30, 1940 and was a 37-year old father, and brother from the Columbia area who was survived by a son, two daughters, two sisters, four step-sisters, two brothers, and two step-brothers. Services were held at Oakes & Nichols Funeral Home, with the burial in Friendship Baptist Church Cemetery in Culleoka. Howell had been charged with public drunkenness.

James Frank Irwin Jr., a visitor who was born on April 17, 1942, was a 35-year old husband, father, son, and brother from Williamsport. Irwin was survived by his beloved wife, two daughters, two sons, his parents, three sisters, and a brother. He was employed as a loader operator for Southern Stone. A family service was held for most members of the Anderson and Rowland family at the Highland Avenue Church of Christ, with his burial in Arlington Cemetery.

Joe Charles (J.C.) James was born on Aug. 6, 1927, and was a 49-year old father, son, and brother from Iron Bridge Road in Columbia. He was survived by his son, and two daughters, his father, three sisters, and two brothers. Services were held at the Mt. Calvary Missionary Baptists Church, with the burial in the Wilkes Cemetery. James had been charged with DWI and driving without a license.

Robert Wayne Jones was born on July 7, 1958, and was an 18-year old farm-worker. He was a husband, brother, and son from Cedar Hill in Mt. Pleasant and was survived by his wife, parents, two sisters, one brother, a grandfather and a great-grandfather. Services were held at North Funeral Home in Lawrenceburg with the burial in Pleasant Garden Cemetery. The charge filed against Jones was grand larceny.

Clarence Langford was born on Nov. 6, 1958, and was an 18-year old from Nashville. Langford had been charged with accessory to auto theft.

Issac Marlowe was born on Aug. 29, 1943, and was a 34-year old from Walnut Street in Columbia. He had been charged with 3rd-degree burglary.

Johnnie W. Mashburn was born on Oct. 7, 1951, and was a 25-year old farm-worker who was a husband, father, son, and brother from Loretta, TN. He was survived by his wife, three daughters, two sons, his parents and a sister. Services were held at North Funeral Home with the burial in Lewis County at the Himes Cemetery. Mashburn had been charged with DWI and driving without a license.

James Harold Marcum was born on Aug. 15, 1938. Marcum previously served as a Private in the US Army and was from Watts Hill in Mt. Pleasant. He was buried in Kentucky at the Pilot Knob Cemetery. He had been charged with DWI and driving without a license.

James Alan Norton was born on Aug. 23, 1958, and was an 18-year old son, and brother from Raleigh, N.C. Norton was survived by his parents, and three brothers. Services were held at the Brown-Wynne Funeral Home, St. Mary's Chapel with the burial in Montlawn Memorial Park. He was one of three inmates who escaped 3-days prior to the jail fire and were apprehended in downtown Columbia, shortly after the escape. He was being held for federal authorities in Florida.

Lee Core Neal was born on May 4, 1932, and was reportedly the inmate who was helping others by giving them wet towels to wrap around their heads. He was a 45-year old disabled Veteran of the Korean War, from Duplex Road in Spring Hill. Neal was a father, son, and brother who was survived by his parents, two sons, and one sister. Services were held at the Franklin Memorial Chapel, with the burial in the Garden of Peace at Williamson Memorial Gardens. Neal had been charged with capias-armed robbery.

Dwayne M. Overton was born on Jan. 22, 1942, and was a 35-year old painter and Vietnam Veteran of Blackburn Lane in Columbia who was both a son and a brother. He was survived by his mother, one sister, and six half-brothers. Services were held at Middle Tennessee Funeral Home in Waynesboro, with the burial in McGlamory Cemetery. He had been charged with public drunkenness.

John Joseph Plaskon was born on July 7, 1957, and was a 19-year old son, and brother from Columbia who was survived by two sisters, a brother, a step-father, and two grandparents. Services were held at Oakes & Nichols Funeral Home, with the burial in Polk Memorial Gardens. He had been charged with 3rd-degree burglary and violation of probation.

Willie Lewis Porter was born on May 30, 1959, and was an 18-year old young man from Frierson Street in Columbia. Porter had been charged with malicious mischief and breach of peace.

William Henry "Buck" Rowland Jr. was born on Apr. 25, 1936, and was a 43-year old hairstylist. He was a husband, father, and brother from Williamsport. He was survived by one daughter, three sons, his father-in-law, one sister, and four brothers. Services were held at Oakes & Nichols Funeral Home with the burial in Polk Memorial Gardens. He had been charged with assault with intent to commit murder, carrying a dangerous weapon, and armed robbery.

Margaret Alice Anderson Kinzer Rowland, a visitor, was born on July 2, 1951. She was a mother, daughter, and sister from Williamsport. She was survived by her daughter, two sons, her father, and one sister. A family service was held for most members of the Anderson and Rowland family at the Highland Avenue Church of Christ. Along with other family members she was buried in Morrow Cemetery in Hampshire.

Stanley Scott was born on Dec. 19, 1951, and was a 25-year old father, son, and brother who served during the Vietnam War in the US Marine Corps. He was survived by a daughter, his parents, grandparents, five brothers, two sisters, and several nieces and nephews. Services were held at Williams Funeral Home in Mt. Pleasant, and burial was in Blowing Springs Cemetery. Scott had been charged with possession of less than 1/2 oz. of marijuana.

Maurice Smith was born on Nov. 28, 1951, and was a 25-year old laborer, son, and brother from Spring Hill. Smith was survived by his two sisters, one brother, and grandparents. Smith's surviving grandmother made arrangements for a service and burial in Maury County, however, his twin sister petitioned the court for possession of his body. That petition was granted, and his service was held at the Smith Chapel Church of God, with the burial at the Meadowlawn Cemetery in Davidson County. Smith had been charged with 7 counts of burglary and attempting to commit a felony.

Dorothy Gertrude Staggs was born on Feb. 3, 1929, and was a 48-year old mother, and sister from Walton Circle in Mt. Pleasant. She was survived by two daughters, four sisters, and three brothers. Services were held at Oakes & Nichols Funeral Home, with the burial at Arlington Cemetery. Staggs had been charged with being drunk and disorderly.

Albert Stanfill Jr. was born on May 5, 1926, and was a 51-year old father, brother, and son from Columbia. He served in the US Army during WWII and was survived by his mother, one daughter, three sisters, and one brother. Services were held at Oakes & Nichols Funeral Home, with the burial in Johnsons Chapel Baptist Cemetery. He had been charged with public drunkenness.

Charles Noble Thornton was born on Oct. 8, 1940, and was a 36-year old house painter. He was a husband, and father from Mockingbird Drive in Columbia and was survived by his wife and two sons. Services were held at Williams Funeral Home, with the burial in Crossroads Cemetery in Lawrence County. Thornton had been charged with violating condition #1 of his driver's license.

Charles Moss Woodson was born on March 3, 1953, and was a 27-year old from Ridley Farm in the Columbia area. Moss had been charged with 3rd-degree burglary.

Dorothy Jean (Dottie) Golden Wright, a visitor, was born on Sept. 23, 1950, in St. Louis, MO. She was a 26-year old wife, mother, daughter, and sister who was employed by Crowell's House of Honda. Dottie was survived by a husband, daughter, one sister, and a half-sister. The Golden family service was held at Oakes & Nichols Funeral Home, with a mass-grave, family burial in Rose Hill Cemetery.

Final Thoughts

It's important to note that when the fire broke out, there were 97 people inside the facility. Over half were able to escape safely. Based on the circumstances, that is truly amazing.

Researching and compiling the information for this book has been a labor of love. Love for my community, love for each and every person who we lost that day, and love for all who were deeply affected by this tragedy.

For some reason, I feel that it has been my responsibility to fulfill the role of an unbiased, and independent, observer who could look at what occurred without pre-conceived notions or agendas. Having no prior relationships with any of the parties involved, allowed me to look at things with an objective eye.

I've experienced loss in my own life and know what it feels like to have a loved one unexpectedly taken from you much too early. The pain is deep, and while it may lessen with time, it never completely goes away.

I also understand experiencing trauma and how our brains respond differently to traumatic events. Experts have found that individuals will take one of the following actions when facing a traumatic event, they will either fight, take flight, or freeze.

Humans, being programmed to fight, take flight, or freeze in the face of grave threats to life, coupled with the disorientation caused by utter darkness, may explain why the eight visitors who were so near the exit, were unable to escape.

While doing research for this book, I've found that much of what has previously been reported regarding this fire is just inaccurate, or at best incomplete. Because of this, I've worked diligently to search for the truth. I've gone through newspaper articles, reports, photographic evidence, and the accounts of people who were there. I believe that I now have an accurate and factual documentation of the events as they occurred that day.

It was said at the time that rescue workers were picking and choosing victims to assist, and favoring whites over blacks, however, the facts show that of the 42 who lost their lives, 27 were white, and 15 were black. Additionally, the last person removed from the jail was identified as Buck Rowland, a white male.

Each rescue worker that I interviewed commented that they were unable to tell one person from another because of the utter darkness and dark soot. The best they could do was determine if the victim was male or female.

Much of what was previously reported about where victims were found seems to have been based partly on assumptions that were not entirely accurate.

Another falsehood that has been told and retold is that the steel doors on either side of the dispatch office remained locked, however, according to the fire investigation report compiled by Tom D. Copeland, Chief of Fire Protection and Sr. Fire Protection Specialist, Wm. M. Steffenhagen, that east side corridor door beside the dispatch office was not only unlocked but it was standing open.

Other reports prove that the door on the west side of the dispatch area was also unlocked, however, the door between the corridor and the hallway outside the primary maximum security area, where Mr. Bellanfant was located, was locked because of the threat of a jailbreak.

Another factor that I must bring out is that many complained that deputies were standing around doing nothing, however, the truth is the tremendous smoke was preventing them from re-entering the jail. The only thing that many of them could do was to step aside and allow the rescue workers, with their air tanks and gear, to do what they had been trained to do. Much like when there is a home fire, the residents do not typically go inside with the firefighters.

The Maury County jail fire did not take hours to extinguish and deputies were never standing around debating on what to do. This terrible event occurred without warning or provocation. The fire itself, other than for one brief second, was contained within the padded cell.

> **The resulting damage occurred in mere seconds, not hours or even minutes. The instant that padded cell door was opened, there was a forceful blast of flames quickly followed by an explosion of dense, dark, toxic smoke, that ripped apart the corridor ceiling, melting water pipes, lighting fixtures, wiring, and more.**

That explosion of impenetrable smoke and soot produced a situation that no one could've envisioned, or been prepared for, however, as soon as smoke was seen, and cries of "fire" rang out, people jumped into action.

Chief Deputy Bob Farmer, Deputy William Duke, Jailer Willie Cummins, Dispatcher Layne Pullum, Criminal Investigator Jerry Dickey, and Jail Trustee Ricky Gillespie all acted quickly doing everything they could, to handle the horrific situation.

On and off-duty firefighters, deputies, police officers, EMTs, wrecker operators, doctors, nurses, the National Guard, the Civil Defense, boy scouts, funeral directors, and citizens rushed to offer their assistance.

Neighboring counties assisted by sending EMTs, firefighters and medical personnel. Fort Campbell Army base sent pilots and four helicopters to rush victims to Nashville hospitals where they would be treated for the severe smoke inhalation.

Many individuals were involved in the effort to save lives that day, and I offer my thanks to them. If they had not responded, more precious souls would've certainly been lost.

The extensive damage caused by the explosion of fire and smoke is evident as the broken ceiling tiles, wiring, and duct work all hang loose. It's hard to grasp the potent force that could've done this unless you witnessed it, or were able to tour the jail to see the damage with your own eyes.

Shown in the following photograph is an apparently weary looking, unidentified male with a soot lined face in the narrow corridor, just outside that padded cell.

At approximately 1:54 PM, the door to that padded cell was opened and that massive explosion of fire, heat, and toxic smoke was released into the corridor.

As visitors rushed out, a call was placed to the fire department. That call was recorded at 1:55 PM.

Sirens from the fire truck were heard as the visitors were seen exiting the jail, and the first responders arrived 90 seconds after the call was made.

Don Martin was one of the first firefighters to enter the facility and he recalled encountering thick, dense sooty smoke, plus an environment with zero visibility. He also said that the firefighters were able to access the corridor by utilizing both doors located on each side of the dispatch office.

As the rescue workers reached each victim, they pulled them to the triage unit set up in the parking lot. Firefighters were not able to identify anything about the victims, other than their sex, male or female. Because of this, all reports that provided the location of where visitors were found are suppositions and assumptions. The one exception to this is the location of Luther Bellanfant Jr.

> **The numerous wild rumors, that are still held true by some, just do not align with eye-witness testimony, or official reports that documented the dreadful events of that day.**

The eight-year time period of lengthy court battles, where the people involved were not allowed to speak about the event, permitted the rumors and falsehoods to go unchallenged, and become what many believed to be truth.

My hope is that this writing has provided some answers to the various lingering questions that have been left unanswered for much too long. After months of intense research, I now see things in a very different light than I did in 1977.

I do have to mention that the interview that I conducted with Phillip Chavez McClarn was profoundly moving. His memory of that day caused me to consider the deeply spiritual aspects of this event, and how angels are charged with caring for us.

As physical beings, we are not able to visually see the angels, but, we can in many instances, see or feel real evidence of their presence, as well as their actions.

While I do not claim to understand the inner-workings of this vast universe, **Exodus 23:20** tells us, I am sending an angel ahead of you to guard you along the way and to bring you to the place I have prepared.

The following poem was written with that thought in mind.

Love is Eternal

My physical body simply fell to sleep, as my spirit was lovingly transported across the veil of separation to a place of absolute wonder and beauty.

As I gazed in amazement at the splendor around me, I turned to say goodbye and saw the faces of you, my dear loved ones, weeping with sadness and pain in your hearts.

An angel took my hand and lovingly said, "do not feel sad, for there is no light without darkness, no rain without the clouds, no physical life without death.

"Many people never truly experience love, however, their tears are a testament to how deeply you were loved. They cannot see you, but you will always be with them. You are etched into their hearts, just as they are in yours.

"Human hearts can feel intense pain, and those hearts mend leaving scars. As each loving soul enters this spiritual realm, those scars tell the amazing story of their life.

"Come now and do not be distressed, for you and your loved ones will be together again. Life is temporary, but love is eternal."

If possible, I would alter our history so that this horrible event never occurred, however, that is not within my ability. I do however ask God to bless our community with true healing, and bless all who were affected by this unimaginable Tragedy in Small Town Tennessee.

References & Resources

Photographs of the scene and aftermath were documented from Columbia Daily Herald articles.

- Columbia Daily Herald
- Corrections Legal Defense Quarterly (1995)
- Maury County Archives
- New York Times
- Maury County Sheriff's Department
- Nashville Banner
- National Fire Protection Assn. Library
- Times Free Press
- The Record, Mt. Pleasant, TN
- The Tennessean
- UPI Archives
- USDeadlyEvents.com

Follow author C.R. Tinsley online at:

https://www.facebook.com/authorcrtinsley/

https://authorcrtinsley.wixsite.com/mysite

Made in the USA
Columbia, SC
20 April 2025

56864325R00085